Designing for People

DESIGNING

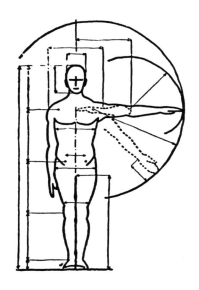

GROSSMAN PUBLISHERS
A DIVISION OF THE VIKING PRESS · NEW YORK

FOR PEOPLE

We bear in mind that the object being worked on is going to be ridden in, sat upon, looked at, talked into, activated, operated, or in some other way used by people individually or en masse.

When the point of contact between the product and the people becomes a point of friction, then the industrial designer has failed.

On the other hand if people are made safer, more comfortable, more eager to purchase, more efficient—or just plain happier—by contact with the product, then the designer has succeeded.

by HENRY DREYFUSS

For Doris

Perhaps the greatest pleasures gained from writing this book were the memories stirred by reviewing my years as an industrial designer. They renewed my deep sense of obligation to my associates who have worked side by side with me. Without their encouragement, criticism, stimulation and, above all, their creative contributions, the work described on these pages could not possibly have been carried forward.

H. D.

First published in 1955, revised edition in 1967 by
Grossman Publishers
Viking Compass Edition issued in 1974 by The Viking Press, Inc.
625 Madison Avenue, New York, N.Y. 10022
Distributed in Canada by
The Macmillan Company of Canada Limited
SBN 670-00392-1
Library of Congress catalog card number: 74-5643
Printed in U.S.A.

Acknowledgment is made to E. P. Dutton and Co., Inc.,
and McClelland & Stewart Ltd. for the
quotation and drawing on pages 230 and 231 from the book
Winnie-the-Pooh by A. A. Milne. Illustrated by E. H. Shepard.
Copyright 1926 by E. P. Dutton and Co., Inc., Renewal, 1954 by
A. A. Milne. Reprinted by permission of the publishers.

FOREWORD

All the world's political ideologies assume that our planet's resources are inadequate to support all of humanity. Assuming either yours or mine, not both, the great nations of the Earth sumtotally appropriate 200 billion dollars annually preparing for Armageddon. Nothing politics per se can do can make the resources adequate to support all of humanity. Adequacy can be attained only by competent design which advances the overall efficiency of humanity's technology from its present 5 percent to an overall 10 percent. At 10 percent all of humanity can be taken care of for all time to come at a higher standard of living than any human has yet experienced. World revolution is ahead for all of humanity. If it is a bloody revolution led by might all of humanity is lost. If it is a design revolution led by right, all of humanity will cross the threshold into an utterly new omni-successful relationship to universe. Moved intuitively by an awareness of this planetary trending, Henry Dreyfuss wrote *Designing for People* twenty years ago. Now we have it in paperback and it should be read by many. Henry Dreyfuss was a founder of the industrial design profession. His book portrays the evolution of a field which has provided a myriad of human advantages.

R. Buckminster Fuller

TABLE OF

CONTENTS

INTRODUCTION

One of our theories as publishers is to bring out the kind of books we would want to read—even if we did not publish them. So, when the manuscript of *Designing for People* came to the office, it became evident after reading the first ten pages that this was one of those one-out-of-a-hundred occasions: to have the first reading of a book I would buy if it were published elsewhere—even in a foreign language.

I had known the author casually, and had realized that he had made my life comfortable and pleasant by having designed a number of things I had enjoyed: my RCA radio, for instance, the Twentieth Century Limited, which so often carried me to Chicago, the Lockheed airplane which, when I was in a hurry, carried me comfortably across continents and oceans, the Ingraham alarm clock, which each morning performed the disgusting job of waking me up with a minimum of aggravation. Here, in this manuscript, I could read at first-hand how and why the author had made those plane rides so comfortable, or why my wife actually enjoyed vacuuming the living room with a Hoover. And it was especially fascinating to realize what my friend, H.D., had done at the Bell Telephone Laboratories to help keep their millions of subscribers happy as well as their telephone operators so uniformly cheerful and tolerant.

As the publisher, I would like to share my all too scant knowledge of the author with the reader of this book. How, for instance, can one man know all those things about engineering, human anatomy, the psychological effect of color and aesthetics on the human soul, advertising, cost accounting and that vague concept of merchandising called "consumer preference"?

There is one general answer to that question: genius. Genius, at least in accordance with my private definition of that much-misused word. A genius, it seems to me, is a man or woman who combines an enormous amount of "know-how" with the purity of outlook of a child. Somehow, somewhere, Dreyfuss acquired a formidable accumulation of technical information in such diverse fields as plastics, theater, industrial production, floor coverings, sound, psychiatry, double-entry bookkeeping, painting and farm machinery. Yet, he has always harnessed this formidable knowledge to a youthful—almost childlike—approach to what makes all these things tick. A shorter equivalent of the preceding sentence can be found in that wonderful word, empathy. For empathy Dreyfuss most notably has—with an engineer in a factory in Dayton, with a housewife on a budget where a dime is far more important than its use as a piker's tip, with a grandmother who is plain scared of going up in one of those newfangled airplanes, with our General Staff in Washington when it became the nerve center of an apparatus charged with fighting World War II.

His biography is relatively simple. He was born in 1904 in New York City and (except for two years at the Ethical Culture School) attended the New York City Schools. By the time he had reached his mid-twenties he had become one of Broadway's most successful stage designers, and was pioneering in the then fledgling profession of industrial design.

When Dreyfuss opened his first office, he bought a 25-cent philodendron plant. Over the course of the next twenty-five years, this plant has grown to fantastic proportions, but it still breathes its air in the otherwise dignified and sumptuous surroundings of the present Dreyfuss office. Henry is sentimental about it and is therefore very happy when clients and friends who know about the plant's history come in and pay even greater attention to it than to the latest blueprints or mock-ups of new industrial designs he is working on.

These, then, are some of the simple facts of Dreyfuss' beginnings. Like most biographies, they omit many far more interesting things that lie beneath the surface. Many of these will be found in the chapters of *Designing for People*. As a background, a report of a few personal characteristics of the author might be in order.

H.D. flies about 100,000 miles each year—mostly in planes he designed himself. His West Coast office is in South Pasadena, about a hundred yards from his home; his

East Coast office is within a stone's throw of the Plaza Hotel in New York. He wears only brown suits, and nothing will make him change. He loves shopping for strange articles in strange stores. He insists on sharing credit for his success not only with his wife and associates, but also with every engineer, executive and advertising man with whom he works on a product. He drinks little. He doesn't smoke, but always has every brand of cigarette available for his friends.

There is no obvious evidence in his life of any hobbies except that of an abiding and intensive interest in the daily lives of his fellow Americans. Thus, he enjoys walking through department and nickel and dime stores to see what people are buying, and reading books—even unpopular ones. He is forever making mental notes of what people like, and sends an endless series of very special, and often very amusing, gifts to friends—unusual flowers, books on out-of-the-way subjects, paintings and prints, phonograph records, special kinds of coffee, menus from out-of-the-way places in Europe with special inscriptions and drawings of his own. He has developed a technique of drawing upside down so that his companion can see what he is designing or explaining from the other side of the table.* He loves the theater, and sees many shows several times.

But, most of all, Dreyfuss wanders over the world being empathic with service station men, ceramic designers, children, animals, proprietors of snack bars, ships' officers, owners of houses, renters of apartments. Perhaps this is why his career, as well as this book, is so aptly called *Designing for People.*   RICHARD L. SIMON

*Dreyfuss made the marginal sketches that appear in this book right side up.

CHAPTER 1.

SOMEWHERE deep in the shadowy past, primitive man, desiring water, instinctively dipped his cupped hands into a pool and drank. Some of the water leaked through his fingers.

In time he fashioned a bowl from soft clay, let it harden, and drank from it; attached a handle and made a cup; pinched the rim at one point to make a spout, creating a pitcher.

Intuitively, this prehistoric man was following the same principles of utility that guide today's industrial designer who creates for mass production.

In the minds of many persons an industrial designer is a brisk, suave character, brimming with confidence, who bustles around factories and stores, streamlining stoves and refrigerators that aren't going anywhere, reshaping doorknobs, and squinting at this year's automobiles and arbitrarily deciding that next year's fenders should be two and three eighths inches longer.

Actually, this is a caricature of the industrial designer. It exists partially because it is only within the last twenty-five years that the profession has come of age, partially because a

THE EARLY DAYS

successful performer in this new field is a man of many hats. He does more than merely design things. He is a businessman as well as a person who makes drawings and models. He is a keen observer of public taste and he has painstakingly cultivated his own taste. He has an understanding of merchandising, how things are made, packed, distributed, and displayed. He accepts the responsibility of his position as liaison linking management, engineering, and the consumer and co-operates with all three.

MY BACKGROUND was the theater. When I was seventeen, I was designing settings for stage presentations in the old Strand motion-picture theater on Broadway, in New York.

Designing settings is an exacting art. It requires a person to visualize and to create a mood. He must be practical in placing entrances and exits and be considerate of the actors who will populate the settings. He must be an expert in stage lighting, the greatest magic at his command in creating a world of make believe. Out of the sheer necessity of pro-

Photos on Page (47)

13

ducing six new sets weekly for 260 weeks came an under-standing of what people like.

I didn't realize then as I do now that my experience in the theater was training for industrial design. In a sense, there was a direct parallel. In the theater my job was to create a set that expressed the mood and the action of the show. With a little strain on the imagination, the producer and the director could have been considered the president and general manager of a client firm. The carpenters, electricians, and musicians could have been the firm's engineers. I had to learn to carry through my ideas, yet deal with these people diplomatically. I had to be precise in my planning. A doorknob had to turn and a door had to open without sticking when an actor made an entrance or an exit. I had to meet a definite schedule—opening night wouldn't wait. My set had to be attractive as well as workable. Besides all this, it had to be integrated into the production. And the final determining factor of success was audience approval, measured in applause—another way of expressing the customers' reaction at the sales counter.

By similar indirection, Walter Dorwin Teague's background in typography and Raymond Loewy's training as an engineer prepared them, perhaps unconsciously, for their rise to leadership in industrial design. There were other pioneers in the early struggling days—Norman Bel Geddes, Joseph Sinel, Egmont Arens, George Sakier, Harold Van Doren, and Russel Wright. In the Midwest we began to hear of Dave Chapman, Jean Reinecke, Jack Little, and Peter Müller-Munk.

When talking pictures crashed through in 1927, the

14

Strand abandoned stage presentations. I was immediately hired by a theater a few blocks away, one of a chain, which decided against complete capitulation to the talkie onslaught.

A short time later the managing director looked at a set I had designed and commanded, "Move that tree!" I said it was impossible to move the tree, although it was a prop. The reason was that it covered an iron beam that supported the theater. He said, "There's no word like impossible," a proposition with which I agreed. Then he said, "No one can use the word impossible to me." I was twenty-three years old. I walked out. Two days later I was on the *Leviathan*, bound for Paris. After a few weeks there I went to Tunis and Algiers. Within two months my funds were gone, and I got a job with American Express as a guide—to make enough money to return to France. On my arrival at my hotel in Paris, I found a great accumulation of letters from R. H. Macy in New York. I didn't bother opening them, assuming they were ads or reminders. Eventually the manager of Macy's Paris office reached me by telephone and asked, "Mr. Dreyfuss, don't you ever open your mail?" The letters were from Oswald Knauth, then a Macy vice-president, asking if I would consider a new kind of job. Would I pick out Macy merchandise that lacked appeal and make drawings in the form, shape, and color I thought would sell better? The drawings would be submitted to the manufacturers, who would be expected to revise their products accordingly. I took the next boat home.

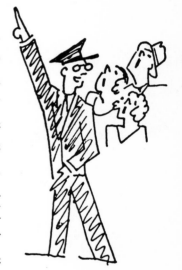

When I reported to Macy's, I made a careful, two-day study of the store's merchandise, floor by floor. A five-figure

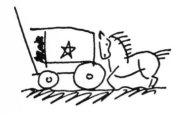

salary awaited my acceptance of the job. I declined. I felt the cart was being put before the horse. The way to improve the merchandise, I said, was to work directly with the manufacturers to learn what machinery and materials were available rather than second-guess them after the manufacturers had finished their costly job. Macy's was friendly to my idea, but wasn't prepared to act on it.

A fundamental premise was involved in my refusal—one from which I have never retreated. An honest job of design should flow from the inside out, not from the outside in.

Out of this Macy's experience, I resolved to become an industrial designer and opened an office, in 1929, at 580 Fifth Avenue. I took on a series of jobs designing stage sets for big Broadway shows to help pay for the office upkeep. Meanwhile I managed to ferret out small industrial-design jobs—a shaving-brush handle, some perfume bottles, belt buckles, neckties, hardware, garters, and suspenders.

These were the depression years, the early thirties, when economic paralysis gripped the nation. Manufactured goods served the purpose for which they were intended, but they came off production lines with a stagnant sameness. When business reached bottom, companies began to undercut each other. At the same time, some alert manufacturers came to the realization that the answer to their problem lay in making their product work better, more convenient to the consumer, and better-looking.

Some manufacturers were reluctant to accept this point of view. They considered the industrial designer merely a decorator, to be called in when the product was finished.

16

They asked, "Can you fix this up and make it look pretty?" Indeed, for a time in this chaotic period a person who knew how to enamel something black and put three chromium strips around the bottom was considered an industrial designer. In time manufacturers learned that good industrial design is a silent salesman, an unwritten advertisement, an unspoken radio or television commercial, contributing not merely increased efficiency and a more pleasing appearance to their products but also assurance and confidence.

INDUSTRIAL design as practiced today did not spring magically from prehistoric man's devising of the cup nor flow from the crucible of the depression thirties. It is a heritage of many people and many turning points in the evolution of modern society. To me, Leonardo da Vinci is a symbol; artist, scientist, engineer, rebel—and the greatest of all industrial designers—he boldly put his dreams on paper. I find it fascinating to speculate about what Leonardo's thoughts would be if he were alive today. Doubtless he would be enchanted by the supersonic jets, but he was not a reticent man and his interest would probably be tempered by his conceit at seeing his prophetic vision come true. Conceivably, he would sit down and doodle a space ship of 2391, which is the same distance in years from today as was his flying machine sketched in 1517.

To pursue the anachronism, suppose he could see the things we take for granted—the small black instrument that summons anyone anywhere for a private conversation, the magic box that by the turn of a switch produces actual pictures and sounds, an immense eye that looks into the

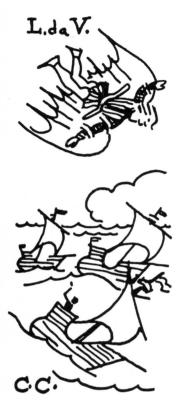

heavens, a glass bulb that emits a light rivaling that of the sun, a destructive weapon that equals an army of a million men, a self-propelled conveyance available to everyone.

One wonders how the brash, imaginative Leonardo would react to all these things, for he seems as modern as today. And then one realizes that Leonardo da Vinci (1452–1519) was a contemporary of Christopher Columbus (1451–1506). While one set out in small, frail ships to cross an uncharted sea, at the peril of falling off a world most people believed flat, the other was recording his detailed thinking of a flying machine.

To look ahead one must learn to look back. Discovering in the past how many dreams of the ancients have come true, we can be hopeful that the scientific prophets of today, with their spotless, efficient laboratories, will be able to dream as accurately as did Leonardo.

In terms of industrial design, the impact that Leonardo's inquisitive mind gave to his era can be related to the chain reaction of revolt in succeeding generations. Strong-willed men rejected tradition where it stood in the way of utility and comfort.

Benjamin Franklin conceived the famous Franklin stove, which heated the air in a room to even temperature, liberating people from the fireplace, where they had toasted on one side and remained cold on the other. His experiments with kite and key, proving electricity was discharged from clouds, led to the lightning rod still in use on modern buildings. He devised bifocals and the "long arm" for getting books off high shelves, a contrivance used in shoe stores today.

18

Thomas Jefferson also had a passion for gadgets, many of which can be seen in Monticello. He built a dumb-waiter concealed in the side of a fireplace—full bottles came up one side, empties went down the other. A weather vane on the roof connected with a compass in the porch ceiling. His fabulous clock that marks the day of the week still keeps time. The large double doors between the reception hall and the drawing room were equipped with a hidden mechanism so that when one opened or shut the other swung in unison. He devised a revolving chair with one slablike arm on which he wrote the Declaration of Independence. He designed an improved plow that won him a gold medal from France.

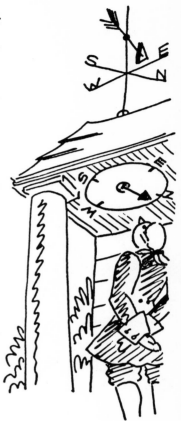

In 1847 Sir Henry Cole, a public-spirited Englishman, startled the Council of the Society of Arts by saying, "Of high art in this country there is abundance, of mechanical industry and invention an unparalleled profusion. The thing still remaining to be done is to effect the combination of the two, to wed high art with mechanical skill. The union of the artist and the workman, the improvement of the general taste of our artificers, and of the workmen in general; this is a task worthy of the Society of Arts and directly in its path of duty."

In 1869 Catherine Beecher, sister of Harriet Beecher Stowe, made a move to wipe out household slavery by publishing her designs for a compact, efficiently organized kitchen. It was well lighted, with standard-height, continuous working surfaces, surrounded by easily accessible cupboards and utensils. Miss Beecher unfortunately was half a century ahead of the day that mass production, new materials, new techniques, new heat sources, and a shortage of servants made her sensible dream the chromed reality it is today.

All these and many more played a part in alerting society to the prospect of better living, but they were only whispers in the wind compared to the insistent demand in the country in recent years for low-cost, mass-produced objects combining utility, comfort, and beauty. It is characteristic of restless, inquiring, never-satisfied Americans to seek something better than what they have. This driving aspiration has made possible the rise of the industrial designer to a responsible place in American manufacturing. His unseen hand has been at work, reshaping the home, the store, the farm, the office, and the factory.

Gilbert Seldes has defined industrial design as the application of taste and logic to the products of machinery. We all know that a machine-made commodity can be awkward or handy, ugly or beautiful. Industrial design is a means of making sure the machine creates attractive commodities that work better because they are designed to work better. It is coincidental, but equally important, that they sell better.

I T IS for the psychologists and the philosophers to determine whether this drive for something better, for more comfort and convenience, gives people a head start toward happiness or contentment. But we can all agree that increasing their safety and improving the conditions under which people live and work are steps in that direction. There is certainly no question that many more farmers today have their ten fingers than they did a generation ago, because manufacturers have put metal guards on moving parts of farm machinery. Some people have a tendency to disparage such progress. They call it gadgetry. But if the industrial designer can help conserve a person's time, effort, and nerves as well as prevent injury he is fulfilling an important part of his assignment.

It was not very long ago that many manufacturers called in an "artist" *after* their products had assumed their final form. He was permitted to add the wreaths of flowers, the bowknots, and the contorted birds and beasts that disfigured so much of our industrial products. This fellow was really a decorator, just one step removed from his china-painting maiden aunt. His monuments were the last generation's sewing machines with their mother-of-pearl scrolls, the gilded radiators, and the lavatories daintily adorned with rosebuds. He's still around, but the beginning of the end was in sight for him when automobile manufacturers reluctantly discarded the buggy-whip socket from their cars.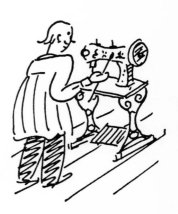

THE industrial designer began by eliminating excess decoration, but his real job began when he insisted on dissecting the product, seeing what made it tick, and devising means of making it tick better—then making it look better. He never forgets that beauty is only skin-deep. For years in our office we have kept before us the concept that *what we are working on is going to be ridden in, sat upon, looked at, talked into, activated, operated, or in some way used by people individually or en masse. If the point of contact between the product and the people becomes a point of friction, then the industrial designer has failed. If, on the other hand, people are made safer, more comfortable, more eager to purchase, more efficient—or just plain happier —the designer has succeeded.* He brings to this task a detached, analytical point of view. He consults closely with the manufacturer, the manufacturer's engineers, production men, and sales staff, keeping in mind whatever peculiar problems the firm may have in the business or industrial world. He will compromise up to a point but he refuses to budge on design principles he knows to be sound. Occasionally he may lose a client, but he rarely loses the client's respect.

IT might seem to some that the designer lays claim to a special omniscience, an infallibility, through which he blithely presumes to offer a solution to any problem. He makes no such claim. He takes pride in a skill based on experience and an alertness sometimes interpreted as vision. He approaches every problem with a willingness to do painstaking study and research and to perform exhaustive experimentation. He is equipped to work intelligently with the engineer, the architect, the physicist, the interior decorator, the colorist, and the doctor. He must know how far to go and when to stop. He must be part engineer, part businessman, part salesman, part public-relations man, artist, and almost, it seems at times, Indian chief.

He operates on the theory that it is better to be right than to be original; therefore, he steers a course somewhere between daring and caution.

If the merchandise doesn't sell, the designer has not accomplished his purpose. Conversely, one of his greatest rewards is the realization that by producing a good design he is affecting the lives of millions of people. And if he designs enough things in good taste, he brings better living and greater satisfaction.

More than any other, this is the reason I went into industrial design.

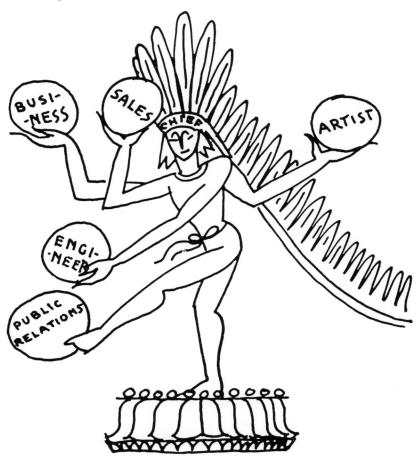

CHAPTER 2.

IF THIS book can have a hero and a heroine, they are a couple we call Joe and Josephine.

Joe and Josephine are austere line drawings of a man and a woman, and they occupy places of honor on the walls of our New York and California offices. They are not very romantic-looking, staring coldly at the world, with figures and measurements buzzing around them like flies, but they are very dear to us. They remind us that everything we design is used by people, and that people come in many sizes and have varying physical attributes. Joe enacts numerous roles. Within twenty-four hours he may determine the control positions on a linotype, be measured for an airplane chair, be squeezed into an armored tank, or be driving a tractor; and we may prevail upon Josephine to do a day's ironing, sit at a telephone switchboard, push a vacuum cleaner around a room, type a letter. No matter what they are doing, we observe their every position and reaction. They are a part of our staff, representing the millions of consumers for whom we are designing, and they dictate every line we draw.

Joe and Josephine did not spring lightly to our walls from the pages of a book on anatomy. They represent many years

24

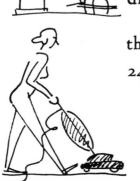
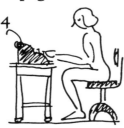

JOE AND JOSEPHINE

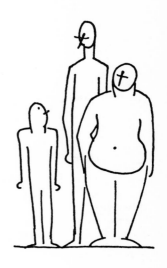

of research by our office, not merely into their physical aspects but into their psychology as well.

Merely assembling average measurements from anatomical drawings would not have been difficult. However, the concern of the industrial designer is with the mass public, and it was necessary to determine the extreme dimensions, for we must consider the variations from small to large in men and women. After all, people come in assorted rather than average sizes.

Joe and Josephine have numerous allergies, inhibitions, and obsessions. They react strongly to touch that is uncomfortable or unnatural; they are disturbed by glaring or insufficient light and by offensive coloring; they are sensitive to noise, and they shrink from a disagreeable odor.

OUR job is to make Joe and Josephine compatible with their environment. The process is known as human engineering. From the mountainous data we assembled, sifted, and translated, we filled the gaps between human behavior and machine design. We have collected detailed measurements of heads and of all the extremities and of thighs and forearms and shoulders and every other conceivable part of the body; we are familiar with the amount of pressure the average foot can comfortably exert on a pedal; we know how hard a hand can effectively squeeze; the reach of an arm—for we must know how far buttons and levers can be placed away from the central controls of a machine; size of earphones, telephone operators' headsets, helmets for the armed services, binoculars—all are determined by our information on head sizes. From these facts we arrived at this maxim—the most efficient machine is the one that is built around a person.

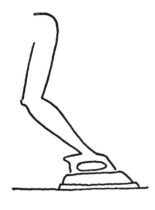

CONSIDER the problem furnished by Josephine doing her weekly ironing. She will spend several hours at the ironing board and unless the iron is "right" she may burn her hand or become excessively fatigued or strain parts of her body.

Before beginning our design, we contemplate the projected iron as an extension or an appendage of the arm. We accept the wrist as a flexible joint and the fingers and palm as a viselike grip that fastens to the handle. The idea is best conveyed by ignoring for the moment which is flesh and bone, which is plastic and metal, and considering the entire linkage as an integrated unit. With this in mind, we turn to our anthropometrical charts for Josephine's bodily dimensions. Furthermore, we know from talking to many housewives that the aches and pains from a hard day over a hot iron are not always in the hand and arm but in the neck, shoulders and back. We determine the amount of heat a hand can comfortably take and develop a design so that the hand is shielded by an insulating plastic. Verification comes from our consultant doctor. And so we set our sights on a light, balanced iron that will not pull at the vulnerable points of potential strain.

If "feel" is of importance to the housewife at her ironing board, imagine how infinitely more important it is in the artificial limbs of an amputee. We learned a great lesson about this in our work for the Veterans Administration. To try to understand the plight of the amputee, members of our staff had artificial limbs strapped to them. The results were not satisfactory. Such is the taken-for-granted magic of sound arms and legs that they were unable to use these mechanical devices. Eventually several amputees worked with us, taking off their shirts so we could see how they co-ordinated their muscles to operate the steel substitutes for what they call their "meat hands." Some of them were so expert they could select a dime or a quarter from a collection of coins in their pockets. These men had trained themselves to "feel." The hook had become part of them, translating touch through cold metal. Through design, the weight of the device was better distributed and it was thus made easier for the wearer further to develop this remarkable ability.

Getting Joe and Josephine seated comfortably at their work presents more of a problem than is generally supposed. For years a man operating a farm tractor was perched uncomfortably in a high bucket seat. Tests showed that bucket seats produced fatigue because only one position could be assumed and undue pressure was exerted under the thighs and on the coccyx. Today's adjustable tractor seats are scientifically developed with correct padding and back supports.

A similar but more critical problem of seating came our way during World War II, when our office was commissioned to redesign the driver's compartment of a tank. Drivers were becoming unduly fatigued, it was found, particularly in traveling over rough terrain in combat. Analysis disclosed that a cramped position was unavoidable because of the way the compartment was arranged. Furthermore, it was impossible to increase the headroom because of interference with the gun mount, and raising the gun mount was inadvisable for structural reasons and because a low exterior silhouette had to be retained. There was a surprising dearth of reliable anatomical information on Army tank crews, but Joe came to our rescue and, with the knowledge provided by our charts, we were eventually able to place G.I. Joe more comfortably at his task. Locating controls within easy reach and making them easy to distinguish in the dim interior was also part of the job. Joe's reflexes played an active part in this phase of the work. In the stress of battle, the soldier must automatically find the right control—it must be in the obvious place, and must be of a shape that is readily identifiable and not to be confused with the lever or knob next to it.

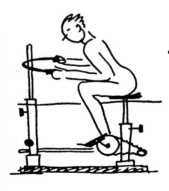

JOE and Josephine have children, and we have charts for them at all ages. They were important contributors during our work on a bicycle; months of study went into the placement of the handle bars, seats, and pedals. An adjustable rig without wheels was built, and children took turns riding it while pictures recorded their posture as the handle bars, seat, and pedals were shifted in position. It was determined that the best posture for cruising was similar to that taken in walking, the easiest posture for racing similar to that taken in running. Movies of children riding their own bicycles to school were taken in various parts of the country. As frequently happens, the films furnished unexpected information. They showed that clothes, which quite naturally varied in different climates, were a factor in bicycle design and had to be taken into account; that it was logical to make use of muscular memory rather than change the pedal motion, and that it was easier for a child to ride a bicycle that was a little too large for him than one that was too small.

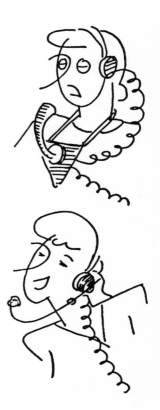

Consider Josephine as a telephone operator. It wasn't too long ago that she had the mouthpiece of the phone strapped to her chest and the earphones clamped to her head. If she turned her head a half inch her voice faded. Certainly there is nothing more fatiguing than keeping one's head in a fixed position. Telephone engineers' ingenuity, plus new materials, provided the basis for the modern headset with its featherweight plastic mouthpiece attached to the earphone by an aluminum rod, which allows complete freedom of motion.

Obviously, the industrial designer has many an occasion to ponder upon the female figure. Such meditation can have humorous aspects. Our first sketch of Josephine was purposely drawn, shall we say, conservatively. The office staff immediately complained that she was the most sexless-looking woman they'd ever seen—in fact, her silhouette looked like a boy. Everyone had a suggestion, mostly along Marilyn Monroe and Jane Russell lines. Some questioned her height, arguing that she seemed too short in stature. It

29

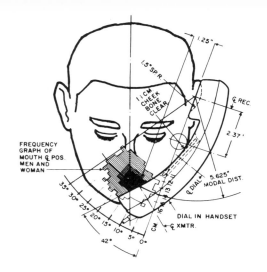

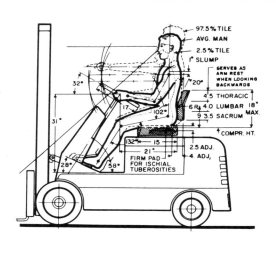

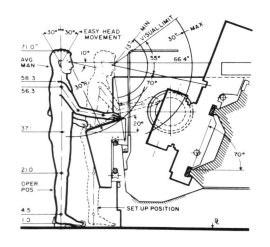

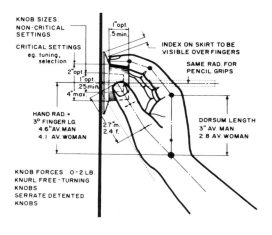

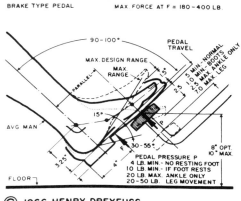

© 1966 HENRY DREYFUSS

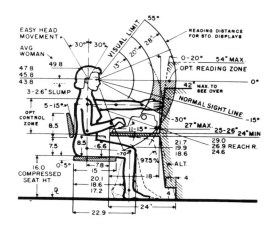

HOW DO YOU START A DESIGN?

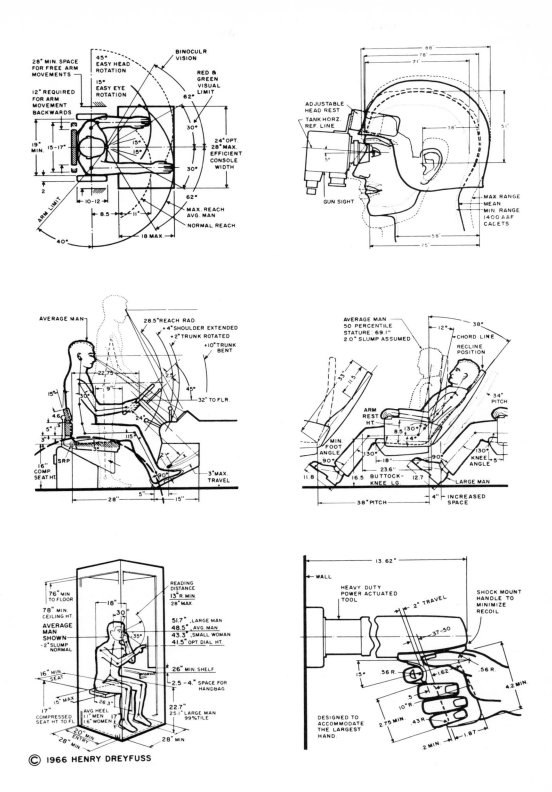

With the man, woman or child who will use it.

We are absorbed in knowing all we can about people—their anatomy, their pressures (mental and physical), their abilities (and limitations) to see, hear, feel and reach during all kinds of activity and in all sorts of environments. What we have learned is epitomized by Joe and Josephine, our percentile anthropometrical partners. And what we have learned is applied to anything and everything we do. We make machines fit people because we don't believe in squeezing people into machines.

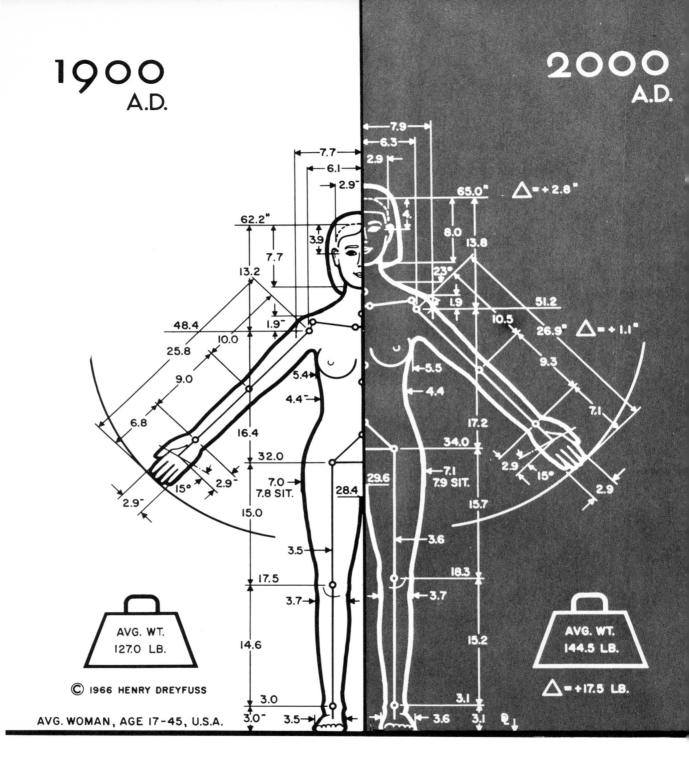

1900 A.D.

2000 A.D.

AVG. WT. 127.0 LB.

© 1966 HENRY DREYFUSS

AVG. WOMAN, AGE 17-45, U.S.A.

AVG. WT. 144.5 LB.

HOW FAST ARE WE GROWING?

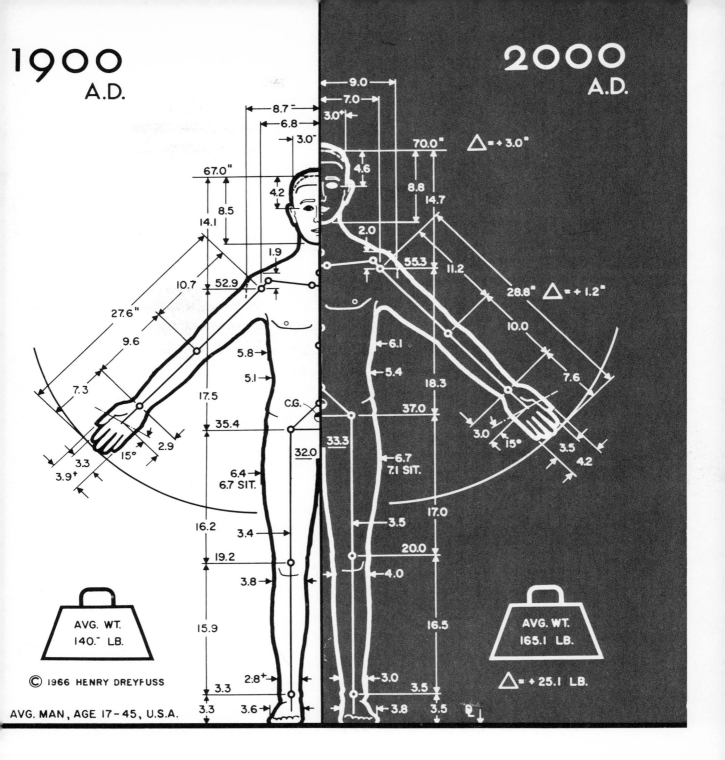

1900 A.D.

2000 A.D.

© 1966 HENRY DREYFUSS

AVG. MAN, AGE 17-45, U.S.A.

AVG. WT. 140.⁻ LB.

AVG. WT. 165.1 LB.

△ = + 25.1 LB.

These charts cover a century in time—with a prognosis for the year 2000 A.D.
Joe grows 3 inches and his weight increases more than 25 pounds; Josephine grows 2.8 inches, and perhaps to her annoyance, adds 17½ pounds.

But their appearance does not suffer, for the additional leisure available permits them to exercise and could produce a race of Greek gods and Amazons.

was decided this illusion was probably caused by the influence of dress designers, who use tall models to enhance their styles. Eventually the chart was made over with increased femininity, and Josephine is now better-looking than the average woman she portrays.

For many years we have retained an outstanding medical practitioner as a consultant on affairs of anatomy. In effect this physician is Joe's and Josephine's family doctor, and often is summoned halfway across the continent to help clients' engineers to determine the proper position and size and shape of a control board or the proper relation of the seating and controls of a tractor.

In addition, Joe and Josephine are also frequently checked by all kinds of specialists, ear doctors, neurologists, psychologists, and opticians, for ours is a preventive kind of research.

How well Joe and Josephine can see is a vital consideration in design. It is matched in importance only with how legible the industrial designer can make what they look at. As with our human engineering charts on the other four senses, we have a vision table. But sometimes mere statistics are not enough. When we designed our first typewriter years ago, our research showed that stenographers often complained of headaches at the end of the day. Irritable bosses could not possibly be entirely at fault, and further study finally proved that the shiny black lacquer used on typewriters harshly reflected the overhead lights directly into the girls' eyes, causing eyestrain and headaches. We proposed the dull, wrinkle-finish lacquer now universally used.

34

IN doing research on illumination, the designer presupposes that sight is a wedge in front of us, like the beam of a searchlight, spreading out from the eyes, encompassing only what the eyes can see. The fully adapted eye has this visual threshold—on a completely black night, when there is no haze, it can see the flare of a match ten miles away. In our civilization such a threshold is rare. The light we mostly see is broken, bent, interrupted, and diffused. Unless an adjustment is made, it can cause nervousness, eye fatigue, or illness. Corrected light can stimulate, give confidence, or induce concentration.

While young Washington read by the light of a single candle, and Lincoln purportedly by the flicker of firelight, Joe Jr.'s eyes are protected. We know that about fifteen candle power is required for easy reading, and carefully arrange it at home and in schoolrooms.

Adequate light is obtainable through built-in ceiling fixtures, and while this is generally acceptable in public places, factories, and offices, we know that at home Josephine usually prefers the warm, flattering glow in the pool of light from a table lamp. Here glare must be avoided, yet sufficient candle power provided.

COLOR can make Joe and Josephine gay or sad; aid their digestion or make them ill; relax them or produce fatigue. It can suggest youth or age. It has therapeutic value in the neuropsychiatric ward and can influence human relations through its use as background in consulting rooms, homes, and schools. There are those who think it can stimulate conversation or create an atmosphere of belligerent silence. It can suggest intimacy or induce hostility. It can make things look larger or smaller, lower or taller, suggest heat or cold. That this recognition of the influence of color is not necessarily a twentieth-century development is indicated by the fact that bibulous English gentlemen of two or three hundred years ago are said to have preferred duck-egg green walls in their libraries, believing that somehow this color enabled them to imbibe large quantities of port without becoming noticeably intoxicated.

Our office was engaged to keep passengers from feeling pressed flat in a ship's salon measuring eighty feet long but of necessity only seven feet nine inches high, the distance between decks. Color came to our aid. By using contrasting colors on adjacent walls and on the ceilings, we were able to create the illusion of greater height in the rooms.

Color has become increasingly important to the industrial designer in recent years. For example, a dark "heavy" color in an airplane can give a sense of security, and a light color can suggest lack of weight in a vacuum cleaner and help sell it.

As a youngster, it was my ambition to discover a new color. I realized that the spectrum contained all the colors, but I dreamed nevertheless that through chemistry or lenses an undetected color lurking in the spectrum might be revealed. I have been outstandingly unsuccessful in realizing that ambition, yet perhaps we have come into a new phase in colors. The fluorescent dyes, paints, and inks that so far have been used mostly to attract a kind of vulgar attention may have more to them than meets the eye. They've been seen only on advertising billboards, Bikini bathing suits, toys, and youngsters' socks. Someday these luminous colors will be used as pigments on a canvas or as a ceramic glaze or to dye fiber in fine fabrics.

For the present, the greatest revolution in color has been the replacement of the utilitarian but depressing and light-consuming black in factories and on machinery by quiet grays. Not far behind is the use of pleasant greens for factory walls. Color experts have little trouble convincing plant owners of its desirability after showing that green reduces eyestrain and nerve strain, enabling machine operators to work more efficiently.

No instrument has yet been devised to measure Joe's and Josephine's color reaction, but we know that their color association falls into a familiar pattern. There is the safety-color code in which yellow or yellow-and-black bands indicate striking hazards such as low beams, stairways, and edges of platforms. Orange or Chinese red indicates dangerous hazards such as electrical fuse boxes, cutting edges, and emergency switches. Green indicates safety and first-aid equipment. Blue tags or signs denote that an object is out of order or is not to be moved. White indicates traffic control and waste receptacles. For pipeline identification, yellow or orange indicates dangerous materials such as acids, gasses, and steam, blue indicates protective materials such as fluids to combat dangerous materials, red denotes fire-protection equipment such as a sprinkling system, and purple denotes costly materials.

We introduced light gray-green in the interiors of military vehicles to replace white. The reasons were obvious—white involves the danger of glare and soils easily. In addition, the white underside of an open hatch presents a perfect target. On the contrary, white is often specified in other situations—for instance, the tops of airplane fuselages, oil storage tanks, and the roofs of buildings. Here white reflects the sun's heat and reduces interior temperatures.

SOUND bombards Joe and Josephine from all directions. Fifty years ago many of the sounds they heard were pleasant—the singing of birds, the movements of horses, the hum of insects. The rise of industry has brought the thunder of rivet guns, the clanging and roar of traffic, and the scream of tires rounding a curve or stopping abruptly. Painful sound registers 130 decibels, thunder 120, the average auto 70, normal conversation 60, but even a whisper registers 25. Clearly there is no complete escape. Noise as a cause of inefficiency in factories costs American industry millions of dollars daily. Great progress has been made in silencing disruptive noises. Heavy machine tools are decibels quieter than they were a decade ago, and modern factories have become comparatively noiseless through installation of covers for noisy parts of machinery and the use of acoustic materials.

JOE and Josephine are affected also by odors, pleasant and unpleasant. Most odorous substances have large molecules, so that they diffuse very slowly. For this reason, smells may linger. For instance, cigarette odor may cling to clothes for six hours or more, musk cannot be removed even after three washings. Odors cling tenaciously to dark materials more so than to light ones, in this sequence—black, blue, green, red, yellow, white. Basic odors are flowery, putrefactive, aromatic, burnt, fruity, ethereal, pungent. The industrial designer must consider all this in his work. The pungency of leather, for instance, can become unpleasant if too much of it is used in the interior of an airplane.

IN pursuit of the correct handle or lever, the average distance a person can reach without strain, the color that will produce relaxation in a waiting room, and other precise details, we have filled our files with valuable data, which we use over and over. We know that pulling force is greater than pushing, that handles under half an inch in diameter are likely to cut into the hand under heavy loading, and handles more than one and one quarter inches in diameter feel fat and give a feeling of insecurity. We know that a thirty-five-pound foot pressure is about right for normal brake-pedal design, with a sixty-pound maximum, and pressure on the accelerator should be ten to fifteen pounds, and that a resting foot exerts six to seven pounds. We know that a circular dial scale, as on a speedometer, is easier to read than a linear one, that a printed page in lower-case letters can be read more quickly than one in capitals. Our files show that from six to nine per cent of American men and four to seven per cent of American women are left-handed. Fortunately, most objects, such as the electric iron, can be used ambidextrously, but sometimes left-handedness can provide a problem. We know that about 15,000,000 persons—12,000,000 adults and 3,000,000 children—have some hearing loss, which is a consideration in designing the telephone. We know that approximately 3.5 per cent of the nation's men and .2 per cent of its women are color-blind, a consideration, certainly, in designing traffic signals.

From all this, it is apparent that the industrial designer's task is twofold—to fit a client's wares to Joe's and Josephine's anatomies, and to explore their psychology and try to lessen the mental strains of this pressure age. It is not enough to seat them comfortably at their work. There is a

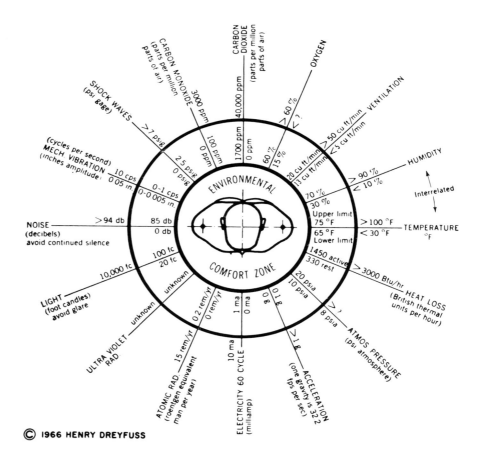

© 1966 HENRY DREYFUSS

How pure is the air? What is the noise level? What does the light meter read? What is the tempe Is there atomic fallout? The answers are of vital importance to the work of the Industrial Designer.

responsibility also to remove the factors that impair diges-
tions, cause headaches, backaches, fatigue, and give them a
feeling of insecurity.

There is little likelihood that their problems will ever
be solved once and for all. Already new ones are emerging
on the horizon. Travelers in jet transports, where the speed
is greater than the sound of the engine, say the quiet disturbs
them. Accustomed to the interminable drone, they find they
become uneasy at the sensation of floating noiselessly,
vibrationlessly, through space.

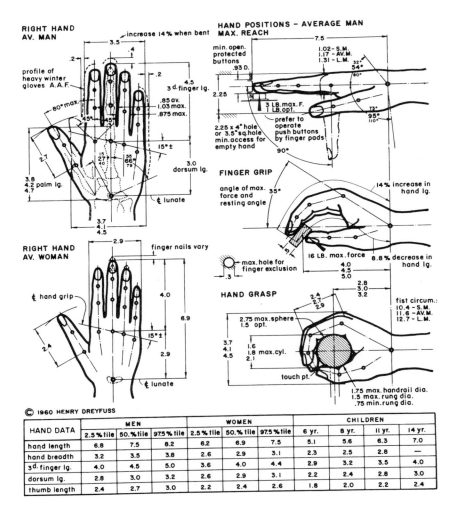

HAND DATA	MEN			WOMEN			CHILDREN			
	2.5 %tile	50.%tile	97.5 %tile	2.5 %tile	50.%tile	97.5 %tile	6 yr.	8 yr.	11 yr.	14 yr.
hand length	6.8	7.5	8.2	6.2	6.9	7.5	5.1	5.6	6.3	7.0
hand breadth	3.2	3.5	3.8	2.6	2.9	3.1	2.3	2.5	2.8	—
3ᵈ. finger lg.	4.0	4.5	5.0	3.6	4.0	4.4	2.9	3.2	3.5	4.0
dorsum lg.	2.8	3.0	3.2	2.6	2.9	3.1	2.2	2.4	2.8	3.0
thumb length	2.4	2.7	3.0	2.2	2.4	2.6	1.8	2.0	2.2	2.4

Hand measurements of Male and Female Adults and Children.

CHAPTER 3. HOW THE

A JOB of industrial design follows a series of steps: When we are summoned by a potential client, whether president, vice-president, or engineer, and he outlines the problems, we make certain, before accepting, that we can contribute positively to his product. Sometimes we must decline the assignment because materials or other limitations would constrict us to the point where we could not be of real aid. Or perhaps the product, in our opinion, may be so generically excellent that design would be gilding the lily. In such instances we feel bound so to inform the man who has come after our service.

Once we are engaged, we request a meeting with the executive, engineering, production, advertising, promotion, sales, and distribution departments to learn their desires, expectations, ideas, and limitations. If we don't all get together at once, we meet individually and correlate everyone's thinking. What price bracket will the product fit into? What new ideas are under development? What means of fabrication are available and what new materials can be considered? We must learn from the sales department what is proper timing for introduction of the product and from the production department how soon they will need the new design to meet the deadline. Those in charge of distri-

DESIGNER WORKS

bution must give us facts about shipping methods and time schedules. The advertising and promotion men must exchange ideas with us as to what features can best be presented on the printed page and on radio and TV.

A thorough study is made of the market. We assemble photographs of competitive products and paste them on boards so that a display of the entire field is before us. Sometimes, to familiarize ourselves with the job at hand, we obtain rival products and actually operate them. If our job is to improve an existing article, naturally we operate it repeatedly. While our clients are cognizant of their competition, we see it through different eyes. Furthermore, it is our job to be familiar with over-all trends that are above and beyond the particular industry with which we are dealing. For example, with the air full of jet planes, the public may be so conditioned to these sleek forms that it will accept or even seek out such forms translated into household appliances. We must make an evaluation of the extent of this conditioning process.

We spend whatever time is necessary inspecting factory equipment, and meeting the men who operate it, to acquaint ourselves with any limitations there may be. We don't want to project a product that cannot be manufactured efficiently.

See pictures on pages 106-107

43

As the design develops we may suggest the purchase of additional machinery or a new method of fabrication that results in a better product or reduces its cost. An example of this occurred when we were engaged to redesign a magazine. The management of the publication took the position that it would be prohibitively costly to use two colors of ink on a single page. A trip to our client's printing plant and consultation with the experts there revealed that the addition of a hundred-dollar gadget to each press would make two-color printing possible. The price was negligible, and the increased advertising profits were substantial. The credit here should not go to the designer. He was merely the catalytic agent who encouraged the plant engineer and transmitted the latter's ideas to management, with the result that a better, more profitable operation emerged.

We enter into close co-operation with the engineers. Our offices become as one. Our common denominators are the same—Joe and Josephine. We go over countless rough sketches. Components are arranged and rearranged. Working drawings and blueprints are made, some by the client's engineers, some by us, and frequently exchanged. Our blueprints, by the way, have letters and numerals on the margins, like road maps, so that any point on them can be easily located and discussed by phone or referred to by wire or letter. Three-dimensional clay, plaster, wood, or plastic models are developed, for we believe that three-dimensional objects should be designed in three dimensions. Perspective drawings are fine up to a point, but they can be misleading. So, as soon as possible, we get a form into clay and actually do our designing in this pliable material. It is from such models that production costs are estimated.

The final model—a working one, if possible—is presented to the entire client group, and with the client engineers we show what they will get, when they will get it, and how much it will cost. This presentation of the final model is the culmination of many months of effort on the part of the client's technical staff and the industrial designers. Often at such a meeting competitive merchandise is put on display to serve as a basis for comparison. This practice, it should be pointed out, can lull the designer and the client into a sense of false superiority, and we constantly remind ourselves that competitors, too, may have been working on improved new designs that will hit the market simultaneously with ours.

We continue to work with the engineers and the toolmakers. Compromises are sometimes necessary, and we consult with them on such changes, agreeing when the change is practical, disagreeing when the change might destroy the conception. A slight change in radius, a new paint texture, and the introduction of screws and fastenings are among the multitude of details which must be watched. The designer must have an open mind and make every effort to integrate changes if they will improve the product or the price picture.

If the product is to be packaged, we design the container, carton, and price tag. Occasionally we have designed the truck that delivers it. We interest ourselves in these matters because they complement the product. In certain merchandise they create that invaluable first impression in the

45

mind of the customer which leads to ultimate purchase. Often, when package and product both are used in display, the package assumes importance as a background and companion piece to the product. Often, too, a package is utilitarian as a permanent storage place for the product; then it becomes an adjunct to the merchandise, really a part of it, and should be designed concurrently with the product.

THESE steps make it unmistakably clear, I think, that industrial design is not something that is superimposed upon a client and his products. Rather, it is a cooperative undertaking in which a group of partners work toward a common goal, each stimulating and supplementing the other. Of the partners, the engineer is the one with whom the industrial designer usually is most deeply involved. In our office we call the client's engineer the industrial designer's best friend and severest critic.

The designer does the dreaming—and it's rather practical dreaming—and the engineer makes the dreams come true. He brings to bear on them a particular skill the designer doesn't have. The final product is a collaborative effort.

Whenever we can, we stress the point that the designer supplements but in no way supplants the engineer. But an unfortunate concept lingers from the early days of industrial design. In that era of growing pains, many engineers regarded the designer as an intruder who was after their jobs. The complaint was understandable. Industrial design didn't have the specific connotation it has today, and these engineers were piqued that an outsider should be brought in "over their heads" to do work that they considered in their

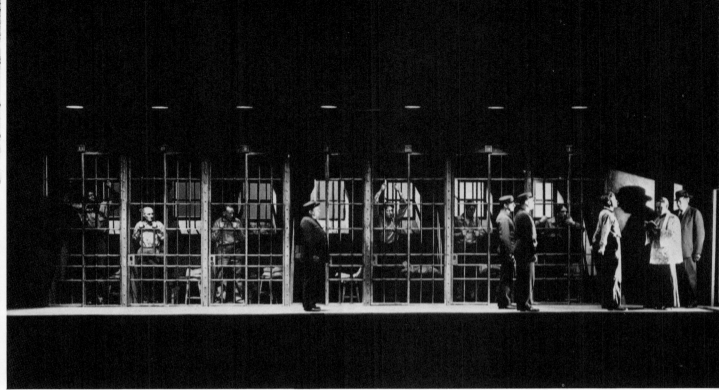

Men came from diverse fields to create the profession of industrial design. The author started as a scenic designer. In the theater the determining factor of success is audience approval, just as in the marts of trade the measure of success is consumer approval. Above is the stark death row scene for Herman Shumlin's production of The Last Mile (1930).

As contrast, the first act finale from The Cat and the Fiddle (1931). The delicate tunes of Jerome Kern required a gay, fanciful atmosphere. As in any successful consumer product or theatrical setting, all the technical requirements had to be met and every detail had to work. And it had to be completed on a rigid schedule—opening night would not wait.

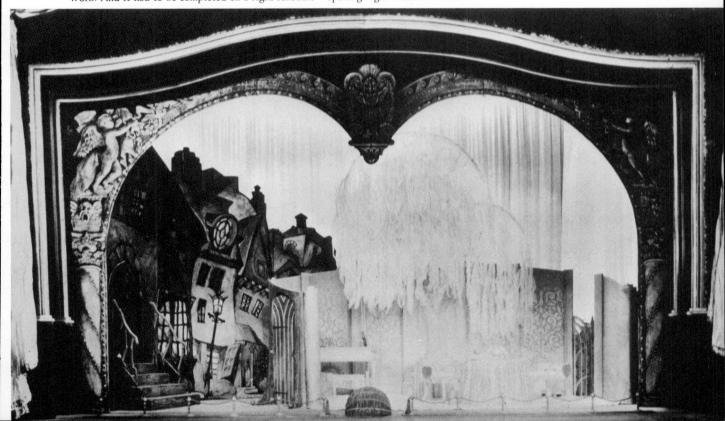

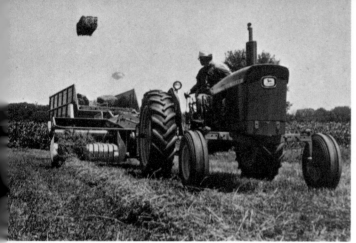
Tractor with baler, ejector and chuck wagon

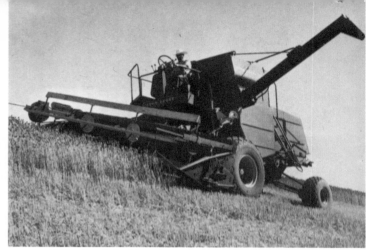
Self-leveling hillside combine

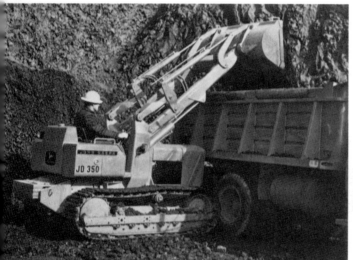
Industrial crawler tractor with loader

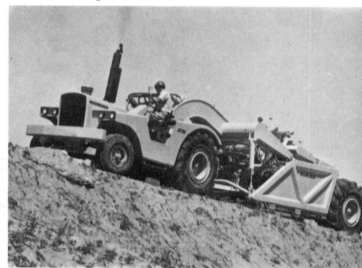
Industrial tractor with elevating scraper

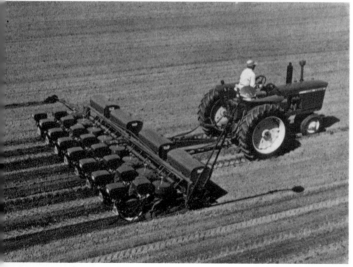
8 row unit planter

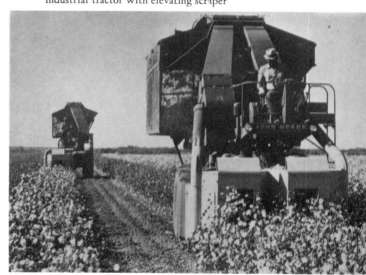
Self propelled cotton picker

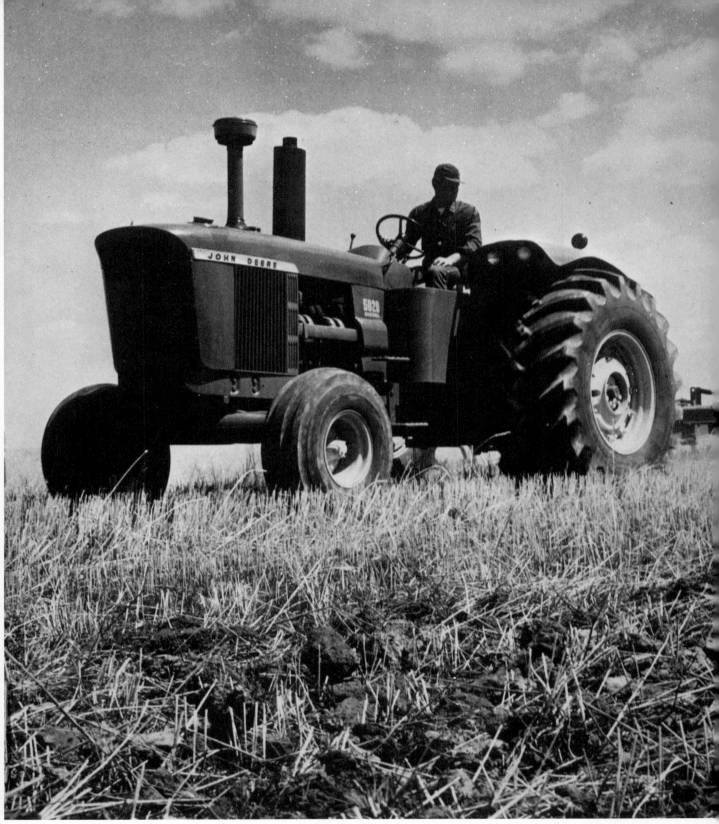

Like the earth itself, and that special breed of men who till and seed and nurture it and reap its bounty, these implements of agriculture have a frugal, rugged, no-nonsense quality even amid today's mechanical sophistication. The engineers at Deere and Company appreciate this and want their multitude of farm machines to reflect long experience: utility, simplicity, durability, safety—and for the men who live long hours in the wind and sun—comfort. Above is the world's most powerful standard tractor—by John Deere.

DESIGN CAN BE TIMELESS...

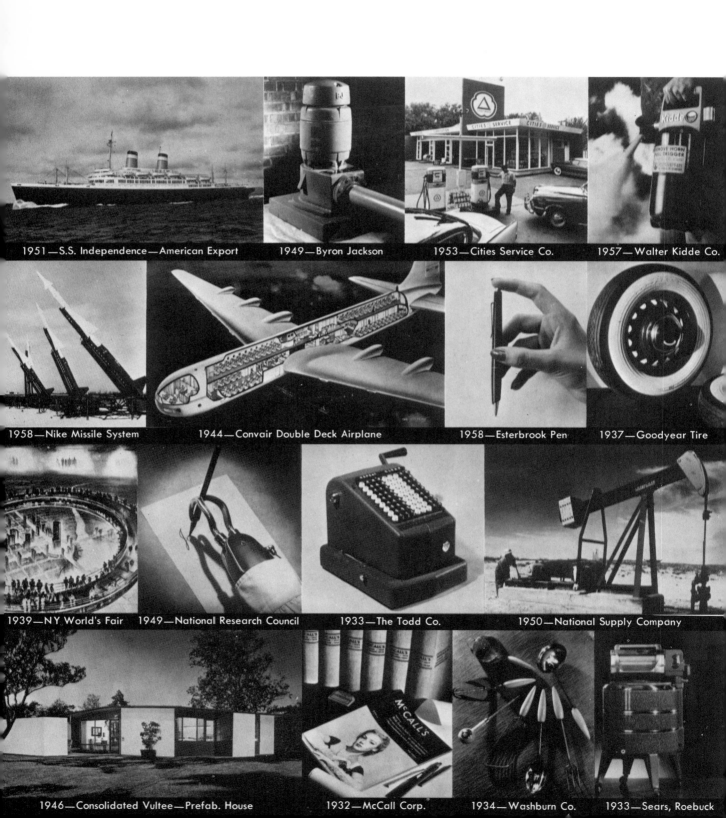

1951—S.S. Independence—American Export   1949—Byron Jackson   1953—Cities Service Co.   1957—Walter Kidde Co.

1958—Nike Missile System   1944—Convair Double Deck Airplane   1958—Esterbrook Pen   1937—Goodyear Tire

1939—NY World's Fair   1949—National Research Council   1933—The Todd Co.   1950—National Supply Company

1946—Consolidated Vultee—Prefab. House   1932—McCall Corp.   1934—Washburn Co.   1933—Sears, Roebuck

Our philosophy has always been to strive for an honest, generic, classic solution to a problem. These photographs illustrate a comment by Gilbert Seldes in an early book about our office. He wrote, "Look on some of these pictures and you will see a clock or a refrigerator or a washing machine which you will say looks more or less like all the clocks or refrigerators or washing machines made today. That is true—but the picture you see here came first. When these designs were made no manufactured object looked like them—they were pioneer designs and they set the basic style in their field."

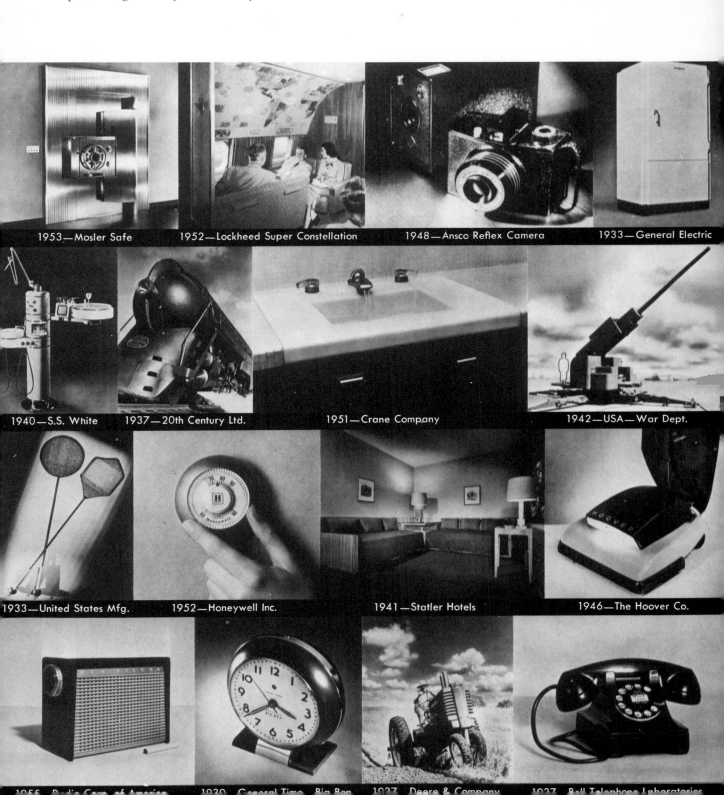

1953—Mosler Safe 1952—Lockheed Super Constellation 1948—Ansco Reflex Camera 1933—General Electric

1940—S.S. White 1937—20th Century Ltd. 1951—Crane Company 1942—USA—War Dept.

1933—United States Mfg. 1952—Honeywell Inc. 1941—Statler Hotels 1946—The Hoover Co.

1955—Radio Corp. of America 1939—General Time—Big Ben 1937—Deere & Company 1937—Bell Telephone Laboratories

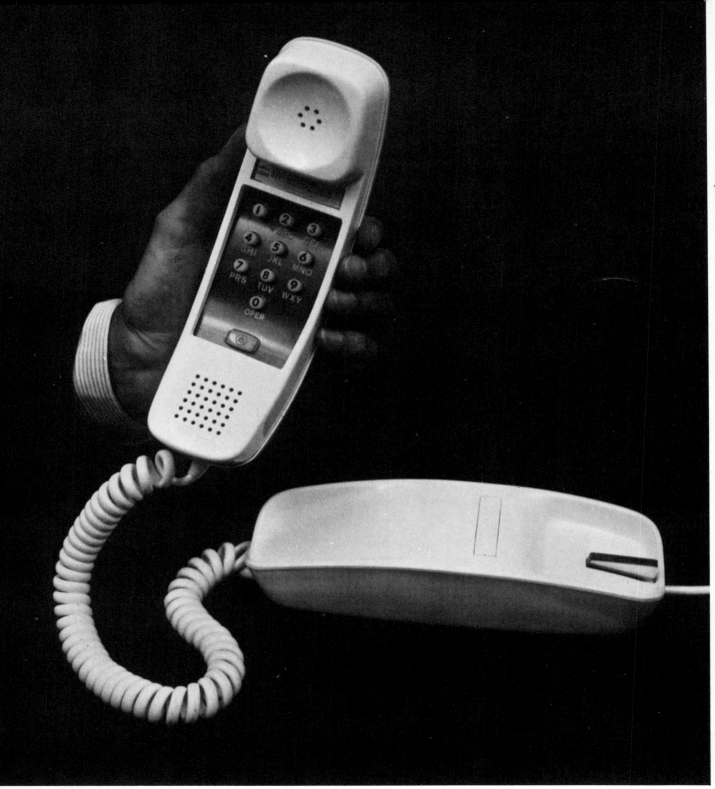

Bell Telephone Laboratories, the research and development unit of the Bell System, was one of the first major corporations to recognize the value of industrial design. Over the years, cooperating with their engineers, the designer has worked on countless products that have influenced the taste of millions. Above is the Trimline® dial-in-handset phone with Touch-Tone® calling. Push buttons in the handset are illuminated to insure legibility.

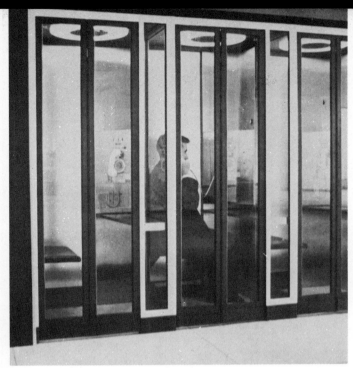

Telephone booths must be adaptable to varied architectural styles. They must be flexible so as to complement rather than intrude upon the architect's concept.

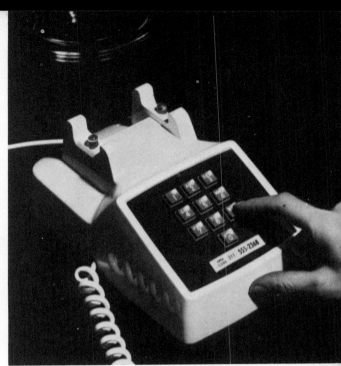

Touch-Tone® is a time-saver to replace the rotary dial. Approximately six seconds are saved in every call; in the U.S. alone that adds up to 162,241,666 hours annually.

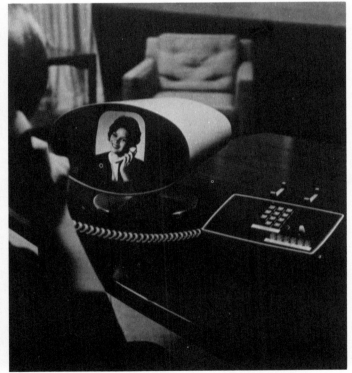

To the voice at the other end of the telephone is now added the picture of the caller. Still in an experimental stage, the Picturephone* visual telephone provides two-way sound and picture transmission.
*Service mark of AT&T Co.

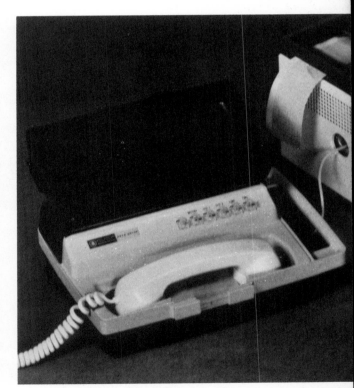

The portable 603 Data-Phone* data set makes transporting the patient unnecessary. It accepts electrocardiogram information and by telephone transmits it around the corner, or the world.
*Service mark of AT&T Co.

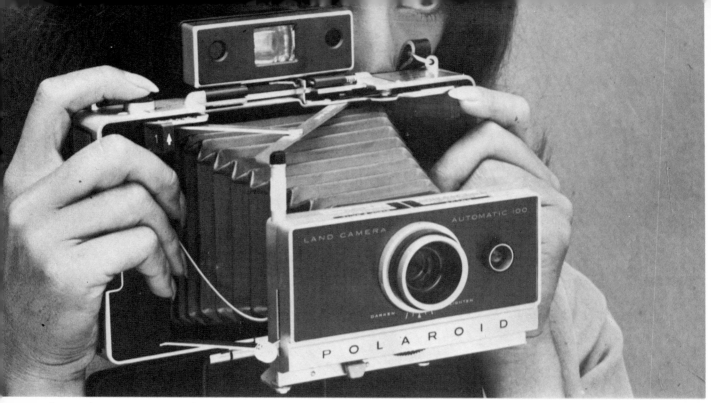

Above is the Automatic 100 Land camera which has opened a new world of recorded vision for ordinary folks. Finished color pictures in 50 seconds. Black and white in 10. An electronic shutter makes exposure decisions for you. Polaroid's laboratory and production staff have perfected the most advanced camera in the world. The industrial designer's concern was to accentuate the qualities of this unique camera.

Below is the baby brother of the line. The Swinger produces black and white pictures in 10 seconds. This economy model spells out a YES when the light is ample, or a restricting NO when it isn't.

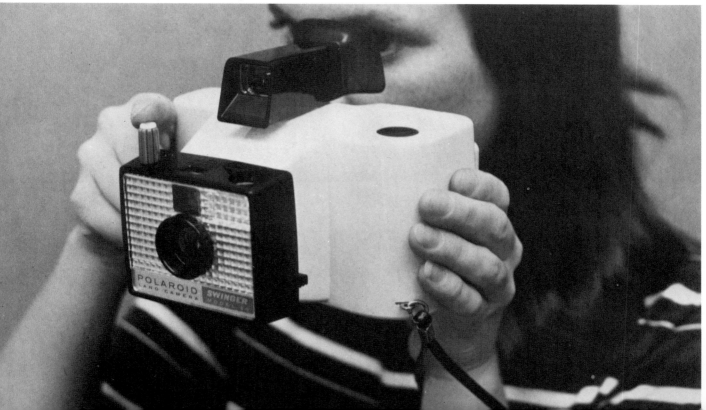

realm. Even today, the term leaves much to be desired. The word "design" is certainly not the exclusive property of the industrial designer. Its dictionary meaning, "to contrive for a purpose," makes it equally the property of engineers, architects, advertising men, artists, and dressmakers. The qualifying word "industrial" doesn't pin it down precisely, either. But it's too late to try to coin a substitute. The term is one of the little agonies the profession must bear. It was therefore a red-letter day, several years ago, when an engineer asked for an industrial designer's help. In this particular case, we had been hired by the president of a company who thought his engineers were not doing a competent job in the appearance of the product. His feeling had been conveyed to them, naturally, and when we came on the job we encountered hostility. Gradually, after several months, the engineers realized we had something to offer and were not competing for their jobs. And when our contract expired it was an engineer who requested its renewal. That was many blueprints ago. Today it is not unusual for engineering departments to be entrusted with the authority to request and to select an industrial designer when needed.

I HAVE often thought that one of the industrial designer's most valuable contributions to his client's product is his ability to visualize. He can sit at a table and listen to executives, engineers, production and advertising men throw off suggestions and quickly incorporate them into a sketch that crystallizes their ideas—or shows their impracticability. His sketch is not, of course, a finished design, but the beginning is likely to be there. Some of us have learned to draw

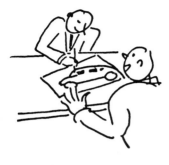

realistically from the client's angle, that is, upside down, so the drawing is right side up from the client's side of the table. I have found this peculiar acquired technique more helpful than amusing.

Equally important is the industrial designer's outside point of view. Perhaps a better term is perspective. He finds himself in a dual role. He is a member of the client's family and at the same time an outsider, retaining his independence and his authority. This is not unusual business practice. The vast and able legal departments of large corporations frequently employ outside counsel. So do public-relations, advertising, engineering, and accounting departments. This in no way detracts from the ability or judgment of those charged with these responsibilities. It is merely recognition that the outsider, because he is an outsider, can be more dispassionate—more cold-blooded, if you please—and cold-bloodedness, industry has found, can be a priceless aid in the solution of a problem.

In developing ideas, the designer makes no pretense that he is a superman or has magic powers. The realm of technical knowledge has become so vast and changes occur so rapidly that no one can digest it all. So the industrial designer consults others frankly and openly. He has learned that the client will respect him more if he admits he doesn't know everything, but knows where to turn for the answers.

Before long, the designer and the client personnel have sized each other up professionally and personally and are on a first-name working relationship. However, the designer must perform a mental balancing act. He must think of the design in terms of the limits set by the client, yet remain cognizant of the fact that he was brought into the picture to evaluate these limitations and go beyond them if it can be established that a better product will result at no additional cost.

Often an industrial designer's work in other plants will enable him to correlate his experience so that he may come up with a key idea that ordinarily would not have occurred to the client engineers. He is also in contact with firms that handle new materials and have invented labor-saving devices and are anxious to introduce them through stimulating new designs.

Many years ago a client who manufactured an electric appliance was persuaded to invest a relatively small sum in a machine to mold plastics. In those days, plastics were not yet accepted, in fact were frowned upon except for incidental accessories. The client went along on an experimental basis—enough to mold ash trays for Christmas gifts to customers. Within another year he had erected a special building for plastic construction and made almost his entire product of the new material.

ALMOST without exception, our designs include an ingredient we call survival form. We deliberately incorporate into the product some remembered detail that will recall to the users a similar article put to a similar use. People will more readily accept something new, we feel, if they recognize in it something out of the past. Most of us have a nostalgia for old things. Our senses quickly recognize and receive pleasure when a long-forgotten detail is brought back. It may be an old tune, a taste of old-fashioned pudding, the odor of a par-

57

ticular flower, the patina of an antique table, or, as in most cases, the remembrance of what something looked like. Somehow these recollections of the past give us comfort, security, and silent courage. By embodying a familiar pattern in an otherwise wholly new and possibly radical form, we can make the unusual acceptable to many people who would otherwise reject it.

A simple, practical example of this may be found in the unnecessary numerals that today adorn the faces of most clocks and watches. I call these numbers unnecessary because children as a rule learn to tell time before they can distinguish one number from another. They do this by memorizing the positions of the hands on the clock dial, and it doesn't make any difference whether the numerals are Arabic or Roman or are represented by dots. Yet it has been demonstrated over and over again that popular-priced clocks and watches without numerals on their faces simply don't sell in quantity. Unnecessary or not, the numbers constitute a survival form that most people demand. Things like electric toasters, coffee makers, typewriters, and fountain pens often bear survival forms that manufacturers think are necessary or desirable. The chrome band on the base of a typewriter is, for instance, a modern version of an older molding, and the stylized decoration on the side of an electric toaster is a modern replacement for the rosebud or fleur-de-lis that appeared on some household article Grandfather used.

The purist is likely to throw up his hands at the thought of such a restriction and accuse the designer of artistic blasphemy. True, we are straying from the path of utter purity when we consider anything but pure form, propor-

You read the angle of the hands.

tion, line, and color, but we have larger horizons than the purist need consider. Ours is the everchanging battle-ground of the department store rather than the Elysian fields of the museum.

FROM eight months to three years are required for a product to emerge from conversation into the retail store, and looking into the future is one of the industrial designer's dilemmas. It's a juggling act with calendars. If his design is too static, the product will be out of date and old-fashioned against competition. If he goes too far, the public may consider it extreme and reject it. The ability of the designer to settle on consumer psychology months or years in advance, and bring out a product that will remain on the market for years because it receives acceptance, has been summarized in a phrase—designer's hunch. Again, this seems an unfortunate expression. It somehow suggests a gamble. Instead, the designer relies on his knowledge of merchandising and distribution, trends, new methods, and how much people will pay for a product. Sometimes it turns out that we do our job almost too well. When our office designed a household article about fifteen years ago, the client was hesitant; he thought it too extreme. Yet, three years ago, when it was suggested that it had become dated, he didn't want it touched. It had been very successful and profitable, and his firm had fallen in love with it.

Too much emphasis cannot be placed on the importance of three-dimensional models. We come to this step after we have analyzed and evaluated hundreds of designs and blueprints, trying to bring some quality to the product that will make it easier to use without increasing the cost, more pleasant to look at without any drastic changes in the factory routine. When our ideas have been formulated, we design in clay, then plaster, finally in a material that will simulate the material to be used in manufacturing the actual product. Wherever possible, such models are done in full size. In developing the exterior of a train or a ship, accurate scale models must suffice.

The cost of a model is more than compensated for by future savings. It not only presents an accurate picture of the product for the executives, but it also gives the tool-makers and production men an opportunity to criticize and to present manufacturing problems. Models of some products can be made for a few hundred dollars. Full-scale models of ship or train interiors can cost many thousands of dollars. A mock-up of a modern passenger airplane cabin may cost $150,000, but it will be worth it, for it permits engineers and designers to develop techniques of installation that would not otherwise be possible. Furthermore, sales executives can bring potential customers into a faithful, full-scale fuselage to see what it offers, long before production begins. It is far more effective to sit in a chair than judge its comfort by a picture of it.

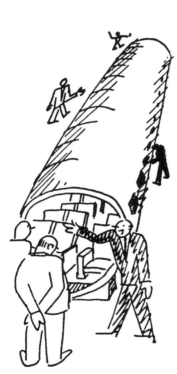

It is always a day for elation when the final working model is shown to the client's department heads. It means that soon perhaps millions of the design, so recently only a brain child, will be rolling off the production line. One of our office's early designs was a washing machine for a large mail-order house. On the appointed day, I presented the final working model to company executives in a handsome,

60

wood-paneled office complete with Oriental rug. With understandable nervousness, I demonstrated that by pushing one control the agitator started. I dramatically added soap to make a tub full of suds. I explained that the next control operated the wringer. Inadvertently, I touched the lever that emptied the tub of its contents. In a kind of nightmare, soap-suds flooded the elaborate room and executives scattered to escape the deluge.

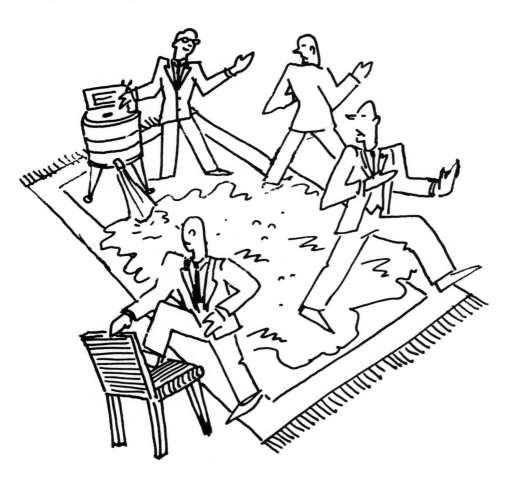

CHAPTER 4. THE

I HAVE washed clothes, cooked, driven a tractor, run a Diesel locomotive, spread manure, vacuumed rugs, and ridden in an armored tank. I have operated a sewing machine, a telephone switchboard, a corn picker, a lift truck, a turret lathe, and a linotype machine. When designing the rooms in a Statler hotel, I stayed in accommodations of all prices. I wore a hearing aid for a day and almost went deaf. I stood beside a big new gun at Aberdeen Proving Grounds when it was fired, and was catapulted off my feet. Members of our office have spent days and nights in airport control towers and weeks on a destroyer during maneuvers. We ride in submarines and jet planes. All this is in the name of research!

Life would be easier, but probably not so interesting, if we didn't have to do these things, if we had a private genie or could invoke some mysterious wizardry to disclose the design the consumer will accept a year or more in the future.

It is easy to look back and analyze the reasons a product sold well and made everyone rich and famous. It is not so simple to appraise consumer preferences while a contemplated article is still a sheaf of "not quite" drawings in the designers' office.

There is such a thing, however, as having a staff whose taste is cultivated and refined to the utmost, whose awareness and sense of order are kept razor-sharp, to the point that

62

IMPORTANCE OF TESTING

planning ahead, always hazardous, can almost be reduced to calm logic. This is not to state that there is any such thing as industrial prophecy; only that the industrial designer is qualified by experience, observation, and research to suggest in advance what a product should look like. As nearly as anyone can, he has mastered what might be called the science of appearance. The process consists of painstaking research, distilling it into its essence, then translating it accurately into the final product. This is what the client pays for and what he is entitled to receive.

Research in itself can be treacherous and misleading. Often people give answers they think the questioners want to hear or that they believe make them appear connoisseurs or scholarly thinkers. Women have been known to vow they would have nothing but the simplest, most modern design for their table silver, then in an effort to create an heirloom buy a rococo pattern that might have graced Marie Antoinette's dinner table.

ONE problem the designer faces is the casual research done by some clients. The client is shown a drawing or model of a new product and promptly calls in his secretary—to get the "woman's point of view." If her opinion agrees with his, all is well. If not, another secretary and perhaps another and another are brought in for corroboration.

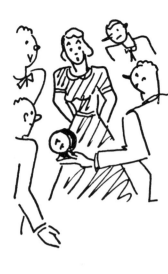

The ladies may assert their independence and disagree or come up with a *non sequitur* to impress the boss or, more likely than not, become so frightened at the responsibility thrust upon them that their opinion is useless. The only result is that the client is confused and the designer thinks dark thoughts.

A client, proud of a new product, has been known to take it home for inspection by his wife or, worse, by the guests at a large dinner party. Usually their criticism fails to evaluate consumer appeal, production methods, competition, costs, and distribution. It's also highly likely that they aren't potential customers.

A client of long standing telephoned me in New York from his Midwest office and said it was urgent that I be at his plant the next day. I dropped what I was doing and got on a plane. In his office he had two models of his next year's product. One was in the color scheme we had agreed upon. The selection was based on the usual careful appraisal. The second was a combination devised by his wife, based on personal preference. Somewhat embarrassed, the client explained the situation but made it clear he would hold me responsible for the decision. Obviously, I had been brought West to play the role of the patsy. Confidence based on experience and research caused me to stick to my guns. The product was manufactured according to our specifications and fortunately proved successful.

Research by trained people is often advisable, with the key questions deftly concealed in a group of dummy questions. In this way the persons whose opinions are sought are put at ease and make no attempt to withhold their true feelings. Normally, the designer works closely with these professional researchers, developing the questions he wants answered and carefully appraising the answers to arrive at the consumers' real desires.

However, there is no substitute for first-hand research in the matter of keeping up to the minute on the sales moods of the public. Wherever I am, I never miss an opportunity to go through a department store, large or small, to study what people are buying and what they are rejecting. I take the elevator to the top floor and work downward by escalator or stair, inspecting each department en route. On such an expedition, the consumers' world unfolds before an alert watcher like a reel of film. Although we do not design in the fashion trades, even those departments offer direction in color and materials. Not too long ago, women who would buy a red dress wouldn't consider having a vacuum cleaner that wasn't black. In people's minds, some things could be radical but others had to be conservative. In recent years these unwritten taboos have been broken down. Colors that used to be considered "loud" are now unhesitatingly accepted in the home. Stores also give the industrial designer the opportunity to compare his designs with rival merchandise. These competitive products could be assembled in our office, of course, but they acquire a different look from the impersonal display of the department store, the clerk's expert sales talk, and the overheard comments of the customer.

BETWEEN trains, I once visited Marshall Field's in Chicago on such a tour of inspection. I had been handling all sorts of merchandise as I walked through floor after floor, and when I came to the chinaware department and picked up a plate to note its price, I realized a store detective had been trailing me. I visualized a long, embarrassing explanation in the manager's office and the possibility of missing my train. Feeling somewhat like a fugitive, I called over the salesgirl and purchased eighteen rather ordinary soup plates and ordered them shipped to my home in New York.

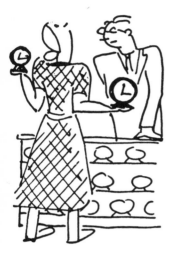

One time I arranged to get behind the counter in the clock section of a drugstore to catch reactions to a new, medium-priced clock we had designed. My first customer was a woman, and I showed her our model and a competitive clock of the same price. I watched her weigh a clock in each hand. I was confident of her choice, for we and our client's engineers had labored long and hard to make our clock light, believing lightness was an expression of its excellence. I had a sinking feeling as she bought the heavier clock. But it brought home the lesson that to some people weight can be a sign of quality, also that the designer must appreciate that some things demand weight and some lightness, and he must determine when each is a virtue.

As a matter of fact, *when* is a key word in the whole business of the industrial designer's appraisal of public taste. The classic example of going too far too fast was the 1936 Chrysler Airflow. Millions of dollars had been spent on tools, advertising, production, and distribution before the manufacturer learned that his car was so far ahead of the public that it was out of sight. Somehow the public's taste and acceptance had not been accurately assessed. The Airflow was not only a major failure and a disaster for the Chrysler Corporation; it also terrified the automobile industry so that engineers advanced with temerity into the streamlined age. Even now many manufacturers disguise good form with an overabundance of chrome teeth, disks, wings, and meaningless shiny bands that distort good form.

Another misfire was the attempted revival of the high-oven kitchen range. Our grandmothers used it twenty-five years ago, but it virtually disappeared when the industrial designer came along and created a revolution in the kitchen by making everything counter height, including the stove. Several years ago, however, research indicated a preference for a high-oven range and a manufacturer offered an improved model. Women liked its greater convenience—it permitted them to roast a turkey or to bake a cake at eye level without stooping—but they didn't buy it. The table-top stove flush with the other cabinets in the kitchen had become such a style factor that the ladies refused to be budged away from it. Today those who can afford the luxury have their counter-top range in the customary place and an isolated oven built flush into the wall at the desired height.

A HIGHLY practical form of research is possible when mock-ups of our designs are built. When we worked on the designs of the interiors of six liners for American Export, we rented an old stable on a side street in New York and built eight staterooms matching the various sizes of those contemplated in the ship. The rooms were completely furnished and made livable in every detail, but were entirely different in size and type. We invited guinea-pig travelers who packed luggage as if they were going on an ocean voyage, some for a one-way transatlantic crossing, others for a three-month cruise, and escorted them to the mock-up rooms. When they unpacked their bags, it was easy to determine if adequate storage space had been provided. From their use of the facilities in the rooms, we were able to evaluate the location of such things as telephones, light switches, lamps, and chairs. We learned much and saved time and money by not having to make expensive changes in the final ship.

A complete interior mock-up is almost standard in designing large transport planes. In addition, we usually request that the same crews work on the mock-up who will eventually install the finished interior. They become accustomed to the design and in the event that changes are ordered they can make them speedily. The mock-up also permits experimentation. One time a whole complement of passengers was engaged to occupy the mock-up for ten hours, the time required for a transoceanic flight. Normal flight conditions were simulated, even the serving of meals. This flight of fancy generated worth-while criticisms of seat comfort, lavatories, food service, storage areas, and lighting —all in time to include improvements in the final plane.

It is necessary to keep in mind that the industrial designer is handed a predetermined area that will be filled to the point of overflowing with passengers as the main cargo. These passengers, some relaxed, some nervous, must be provided with all the conveniences of home, with innumerable safety devices, diversion, food, luggage and clothing space, and possibly facilities for the family cat. After all the information is compiled, the designer goes to work on the jigsaw puzzle, devising the most practical and attractive interior layout. He evaluates every conceivable arrangement of the components for using the limited space to the best advantage. The best of these are ultimately presented to the client for comment or approval and the most feasible plan is adopted.

INFORMATION of another sort was obtained when two men from our office were assigned to ride commercial air liners back and forth across the country to gauge actual passenger reaction, preparatory to designing a new transport. Their unseen companions were Joe and Josephine, who always go along when there's testing to be done.

Among other things, the research men discovered that many gadgets in a plane do not operate in a manner to which the passenger is accustomed, particularly if the appearance does not immediately explain the function. A United Air Lines' stewardess told them that passengers occasionally drop letters into the air-conditioning slots on a DC-6 in the belief that they are for mail. A stewardess on a TWA Constellation reported that babies are sometimes tucked into the overhead rack by unknowing mothers. Some passengers can't tell one end of the plane from the other in flight and ask, "Which is the front end?" "Which way are we going?" Passengers are baffled by lavatory door latches, tricky soap dispensers, and water taps. Hence a rule we follow: design should be obvious. We consciously avoid hidden controls or concealed handles on everything we do. If a door or a panel is supposed to open, we try through design to show how it opens. If something is to be lifted or operated by a handle, we try to integrate the lifting device into the design, but never to conceal it. At the expense of forfeiting originality, and it is a great temptation to hide locks and access panels, we try to make things obvious to operate, not only in airplane interiors but in everything we do.

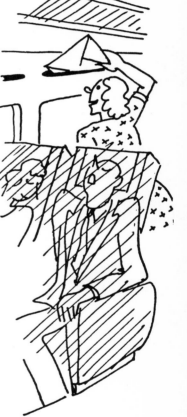

CHAPTER 5. THROUGH

THE years are good for us. For the most part, the best of the past has survived, with the result that the present generation enjoys a heritage of beauty and comfort. Occasionally an era of bad taste disturbs this heritage, but time and the surge of civilization edit it out.

The magnificent art works of the early Chinese dynasties, the architecture and artifacts of the ancient Egyptians and the Greeks, are faithful records of the cultures of their times, as is the so-called primitive art that comes from Africa and the South Seas and from that whole civilization represented by the term "pre-Columbian."

Early applied decoration might be termed "agricultural ornament," for it is easy to see that it was inspired by the straight lines that the plow or digging stick made in the earth; one sees the zigzag and even the curve of what was the forerunner of contour plowing. The checkerboard type of decoration is a reflection of the tilled square of ground. One often comes across symbols of fertility as decoration —early abstractions depicting seeds and young bamboo shoots. Such decoration was related to the actual experiences of early man's life.

As time went on, the growing complexity of society was

THE BACK DOOR

reflected in more complex forms, but even more in the contrived patterns applied to them. The simple treatment inspired by the furrows in the soil became more refined and the original concept was lost as the lines resulted in Chinese geometric patterns and in the Greek frieze.

In Western civilization, the culmination was reached in the early medieval cathedrals of Europe. Decoration was rich but always subservient to form. To this day the cathedrals of the era, with their superb sculpture and stained glass, represent a magnificent blending of art and architecture.

During the Renaissance and post-Renaissance, when urban development produced an air of luxury and richness, there was an ever-increasing tendency toward overdecoration—to a point where the original form was lost and the function obscured. Doors were encrusted with carving and painting, so that sometimes it was difficult to tell where they would open. Walls, ceilings, floors, and the leaded- and stained-glass windows of the time were a mass of voluptuous decoration. Even the outstanding work of that day, Michelangelo's ceiling in the Sistine Chapel, was confused by his own framework of simulated architecture and was surrounded by a superabundance of paintings by other artists. Perhaps there were too many artists and crafts-men and not enough buildings and objects to go around. More likely, the reckless, unrestrained adornment was an expression of the exuberant living and the intrigue of the period.

Later came the frenzied overdecoration of the baroque and rococo. Granted that occasionally this plaster era pro-duced a breath-taking interior; for the most part, it was a question whether the architects of Paris and old Vienna were inspired by the pastry cooks or vice versa!

Then for a brief period there was the relief of Sheraton and the Adamses, who developed their styles with simple grace along neoclassic lines.

Always through the darkness shines the purity of design of homes and furnishings indigenous to the country that produced them. In America in the eighteenth century some of the results were outstanding. Consider the fine simplicity and functionalism of a Shaker settee or the elegance of a Windsor chair, the well-considered placing of small win-dows in a clapboard house, or the well-proportioned and unadorned chimneys.

From the time of the First Empire through the reign of Victoria, nothing was left untouched. Decoration de-scended on every article in view. Chairs had dismembered lion's claws for legs and roses carved along the backs. The living room was a jungle in which flowers grew wild, animals stampeded, and horns of plenty burst open. What wasn't carved was overstuffed and bloated.

Around the turn of the century came an abortive effort to get free of traditional forms. Flowers and trees and vines tried to dance a ballet more graceful than nature itself. They called it *l'art nouveau*. One can see it in the stations of the Paris *Métro* but little more of it remains today. It was an unsuccessful attempt to break away from the eclecticism of the time.

At the same time a feeling for functionalism was stirring in certain areas abroad, and to make it more palatable there appeared in the 1920's a gaudy transitional period when chromium bands and borders, flamboyant sunbursts, and contorted flowers were tossed together to produce a salad reminiscent of some of the worst of rococo. Recall the interiors aboard the *Ile de France*. Traces of this era of design linger in a few places, but once the reaction set in, it was comparatively swift and devastating. Decoration largely disappeared and functionalism took hold in the objects around us.

At first, as in medieval days, the wealthy employed individual craftsmen to rescue them from the maze. Groups of artists and craftsmen such as the Bauhaus in Germany integrated their arts and produced forms not derivative from nature but adjusted to the restrictions of the tools and machines that would make them, and they took into consideration the new materials and methods of fabrication that were available. (The Nazis, with their unrefined hankering for what they thought was a lost *Kultur*, put a stop to this new school of thought. Only lately has a recovery been apparent in Germany.)

73

The French developed simple basic forms, but added stylized floral and animal decorations.

In the Scandinavian countries craftsmen were developing designs in furniture, glass, fabrics, and silver of a rare quality.

All these new designs were the efforts of individual craftsmen, with their limited output, so that only a few of the privileged could enjoy liberation from the lion's claws and the creeping scrolls. It remained for the United States, with its vast mass production, to carry the mood for simplicity into every household in the nation. Spearheading this move were the handful of dedicated men who formed the nucleus of the new profession, industrial design. They combined the temperament of the craftsman with a new concept of craftsmanship, that of bringing it to the mass public. To accomplish this they set out to explore the mass mind, the market, machinery, and materials.

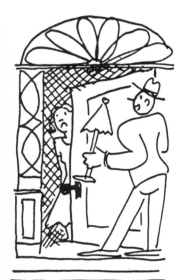

IT WAS not surprising that when they tried to introduce their new designs into the sacred American living room they were rebuffed at the front door. But they persisted and finally gained entrance through the back door. Their first achievements were in the kitchen, the bathroom, and the laundry, where utility transcended tradition.

From the back door to the front of the house—and thence into the whole world outside—turned out to be a comparatively short route for the pioneer industrial designers. Unfortunately, their inexperience led them into strange detours during those early days. As if under a spell, they

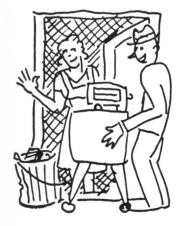

74

accepted the half-truth of streamlining. Hearses and fountain pens and pencil sharpeners were stupidly modeled after the teardrop, which was held up as an ideal form, one which a body free to change its shape would assume, in order to offer a minimum of resistance to air. Some critics pointed out that fountain pens and the baby buggies seldom stirred up much of a breeze, and a streamlined pencil sharpener couldn't get away if it tried because it was screwed down, but the critics were readily outshouted.

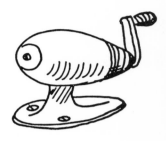

Needless streamlining was made even more ridiculous when high-speed photography revealed that the teardrop form was an optical illusion, that falling drops of water assume all kinds of impractical, air-resisting shapes as they tumble through space. The specter still haunts industrial design, for some manufacturers still find that "streamlining" sells products, despite twenty years of scoffing by engineers and aesthetes. But out of the era of so-called streamlining, the designer learned a great deal about clean, graceful, unencumbered design. He learned to junk useless protuberances and ugly corners that not only spoiled good honest lines but interfered with efficient operation. Stand a 1929 toaster with its knobs and knuckle-skinning corners and impossible-to-clean slits and over-all ugliness next to today's model, and the difference is apparent. The designer was in the right stable but on the wrong horse. Call it clean-lining instead of streamlining, and you have an ideal that the designer today still tries to achieve.

There is a tendency to think of functional form in terms of superstreamlining, jet propulsion, and chromium tubing. I have a homely reminder for those who do. Years ago, as competition began to catch up, the manufacturers of the round Mason jars sought a change. Here was a temptation to prettify a familiar object. Happily, we resisted it. We made the jar square with tapered sides, thereby giving the consumer a saving in storage space, providing a jar that wouldn't roll off the kitchen table, and handing the manufacturer a thumping sales advantage. It was another lesson in the basic simplicity of good design.

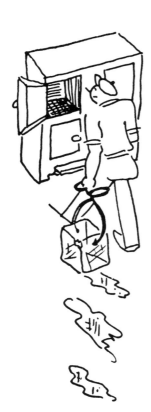

About this time, there were faint stirrings in the direction of modernizing the kitchen, but housewives were not yet in outspoken revolt. Perhaps they were too tired. They were putting up with inefficient kitchens and bathrooms because there was nothing else they could do. Remember, the country was still emerging from the pink-silk-lampshade-with-beaded-fringe era. Recall, if you will, the stove with the fancy protruding legs. Someone felt that they were not just supports; they had to be decorated with cast-iron scrolls. Recall, also, the paneled golden-oak ice chest on the back porch, requiring many tiring steps to reach, and the iceman tracking in mud and dripping water when he replenished the supply, and the pan underneath that overflowed when someone forgot to empty it. There were the sink that was impossible to clean, the poor lighting and ventilation, the cupboard doors that would never catch, and the inaccessible, dirt-catching corners.

Things were much the same in the bathroom. No one knows for sure why bathtubs were set on iron claw legs, forming a difficult dirt pocket underneath. Nor why ceramic basins were cemented under a hole in a marble slab, form-

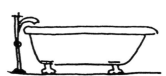

ing a hidden grease pocket around the joint. Today most people do their own housework, and when we undertake a bathroom-design assignment we want to know how easily it can be kept clean, maintained, and repaired. In the improved basin, the faucets and handles with their inaccessible, dirt-catching undersurfaces have been replaced by rounded valves, put in from the top and set on ceramic pads that are easy to clean.

See page 51

The back-porch soapstone washtub and the knuckle-skinning washboard and the large, unwieldy bar of soap can be recalled only with a shudder, and perhaps a psychosomatic twinge in the sacroiliac in memory of the aching backs women acquired in this slavery. The early-day electric washing machine was a great step ahead, but it almost seemed that the manufacturer was trying to prove how inconveniently he could scatter the controls. It was an imposition on womankind compared to today's washer, with its automatic washing, rinsing, and damp drying.

HABIT is a powerful force. At first many housewives were reluctant to give up their inefficient kitchens. They were accustomed to the old stove, the old sink, and the old toaster. They were somewhat like the president of a company that manufactured a familiar instrument of torture, the dental unit, the old one that had the spittoon, drill, worktable and light, each supported on a contorted, striped cast-iron arm. He came to me and asked what was wrong with his product, which had sold successfully for many years. I told him it looked like a tree. He asked, "What's wrong with a tree?" He had me there. Nevertheless, he engaged our office to aid in designing a new unit. It is the neat, compact cylinder now generally seen in dentists' offices. Gas, electricity, air pressure, water supply, sewage disposal, and X-ray camera are all integrated in it. When he first saw it, he said with a twinkling eye, "It looks like a gasoline pump." I said, "What's wrong with a gasoline pump?" I had him there.

Turn to page 51

Once started, the metamorphosis in the bathroom, laundry, and back porch was accomplished rather easily. The housewife was glad to discard the old bathtub and the back-straining washtub and the troublesome old oak icebox. But the kitchen was another matter. Moving Grandma's rocker from its traditional spot near the window meant breaking a strong sentimental tie. However, in this case utility overrode sentiment. To a woman who spends one-fourth of her day in the kitchen, there is no sales talk so eloquent as a modern refrigerator or stove or sink that is convenient to use and easy to keep clean.

TREMENDOUS impetus was given this quarter-century evolution from dark, helter-skelter, inefficient utility rooms to the kind of kitchen to be seen in today's household magazines, movies, and television, by two things that had nothing to do with cooking a meal or taking a bath—the automobile and the airplane. They represent progress in a way that nothing else does. Actually, the auto and the plane have become symbols of the nation's scientific imagination and a vital part of its psychology, establishing trends and influencing people in everything they buy.

It has been said that, having entered through the back

78

door, the industrial designer rode into the living room on the mobile vacuum cleaner, to carry on and complete his invasion of the home. The results are a proud display, both by the merchant and the homeowner. Twenty years ago, it was impossible to buy good, mass-produced contemporary furniture and household accessories. Today, a home in excellent taste can be furnished from almost any department store or from a Sears Roebuck or Montgomery Ward catalogue.

Household appliances have become so glamorous that it is not unusual for a husband to give his wife a gaily be-ribboned new vacuum cleaner or refrigerator for her birthday or Christmas. Can you imagine our grandmothers finding a new broom or an oak icebox under their Christmas trees, gifts from our grandfathers?

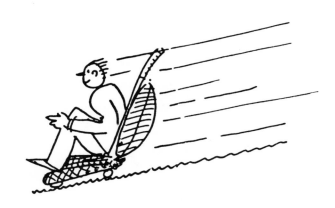

CHAPTER 6. RISE IN THE

FREQUENTLY I hear people say, with or without intended snobbery, that Americans are so engrossed in materialistic values that culture is lost on them. The most obscure European peasant, these people say, has a greater appreciation and understanding of the arts than most Americans. He enjoys the opera and the art galleries, the refrain goes, and doesn't need a houseful of gadgets to enjoy life.

They imply that Americans, in their worship of comfort and luxury, have so surrounded themselves with slick mechanization that their capacity to esteem the fine arts has become dulled or has disappeared entirely.

It would be futile to argue with these people, for their point of view grows out of a complete misunderstanding of what is going on in this country. They fail to appraise the direction that public appreciation of the arts has taken here.

It is my contention that well-designed, mass-produced goods constitute a new American art form and are responsible for the creation of a new American culture. These products of the applied arts are a part of everyday American living and working, not merely museum pieces to be seen on a Sunday afternoon.

LEVEL OF PUBLIC TASTE

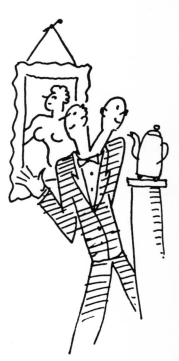

I find no basic conflict between those who appreciate the fine arts and those who respond to classic examples of the applied arts. They are stirred by the same impulse, a desire for beauty.

For many years appreciation of the arts was limited to the privileged classes. Except for the impact of the church, where awe really supplanted appreciation, the average man rarely came in contact with beauty other than the ever-present beauty of nature. He had no access to fine paintings, sculpture, and furnishings. These were the exclusive property of wealthy patrons. Ironically enough, there have been times when the arts and crafts have sunk to so low a level of taste that it's questionable which was the privileged class—those who surrounded themselves with the contorted forms the era dictated or the impoverished man in his cottage, forced to use simple, inexpensive, and therefore undecorated utilitarian objects.

Another part of the diatribe about uncultured Americans has to do with the so-called evils of big business and the system of mass production it has developed. There is, of course, another side of that coin. Big business and mass production have created countless benefits for the people of this country, not the least of which is the amazing rise in the level of public taste through good design of consumer products.

Public taste, as used here, embraces a heterogeneous mass of people, not any particular income group or educational level. Some will be moved by a Van Gogh, others will feel elation at the sight of a sleek jet plane. Exposure to a fine piece of sculpture is likely to create in a person an awareness of the excellent lines of a thermos jug or a lamp, and vice versa. Thus, when a good design is mass-produced, its influence is tremendous. This impact will be translated into an improvement in people's taste when they go shopping. Unconsciously, a person's contact with beauty quickens and heightens his perception and taste for all forms of art.

We discovered this when we worked on two hundred railway passenger coaches, one of our jobs for the New York Central System. When the estimates came in, the budget had to be revised to reduce costs. One of the first things eliminated were the mirrors for the bulkheads at both ends of each car. The thought of those blank areas was disturbing, and we hit upon the idea of relieving their starkness with fine reproductions of great works of art. I have always felt that the railroad officials were merely pleasing my fancy in permitting us to turn their luxurious new coaches into a kind of art gallery. But they permitted us to go ahead gathering the necessary four hundred prints and arranging entire trains exhibiting everything from Rembrandts to Picassos. Little did we realize what we were getting in for. The first week the trains were in operation, more than one thousand com-

82

plimentary letters were received from pleased passengers, many of them requesting information as to where copies of these reproductions could be obtained.

As the weeks passed, the mail multiplied, and eventually the railroad officials, precipitated into the uncomfortable role of art connoisseurs, brought out a descriptive brochure with the rather grand title, "Art on Wheels."

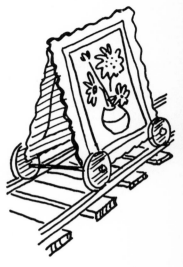

THE awakening of the American people to painting in the last few years has been unprecedented. Thousands of persons who uncritically "only knew what they liked" have learned about Rembrandt and Cézanne. Much of the credit for this stimulus must go to *Life* magazine, which regularly reproduces outstanding examples of paintings, sculpture, cathedrals, fine tapestries, and the like, and has met an enthusiastic response from its diversified audience. This interest has spread. Doctors recommend painting as therapy for hypertension. Every large city has businessmen art groups who paint for pleasure. After all, the leading citizens in both London and Washington are week-end painters. People stood in line and paid an admission fee to see a collection of famous European works of art sent on a nation-wide tour. One of the most popular covers ever published by the *Ladies Home Journal* was a reproduction of Van Gogh's *Sunflowers*. Fine works have been shown on television with commentaries by competent critics. Significantly, TV audiences are not offended by seeing some such priceless object as the Cellini cup and, a few minutes later, a well-designed automobile or refrigerator.

It may surprise many to learn that almost as many people

attended New York City's museums in 1954 as attended the leading sports arenas in that city.

Attendance at the museums was as follows:

American Museum of Natural History	2,218,565
Brooklyn Museum	429,797
Cloisters	702,857
Frick Museum	131,843
Metropolitan Museum of Art	2,131,418
Museum of the City of New York	135,293
Museum of Modern Art	528,807
Whitney Museum	99,456
Other museums in City limits	201,050
	6,579,086

Attendance at athletic events:

Madison Square Garden	3,409,000
Ebbetts Field	1,022,581
Polo Grounds	1,155,169
Yankee Stadium	1,475,171
	7,061,921

The evidence also shows that the American people will listen to good music, if given the chance. Approximately 3,000,000 people listen to the NBC Symphony each week on radio—more than could hear it in Carnegie Hall in a hundred years. Four million hear the Telephone Hour on radio. When Menotti's opera *Amahl and the Night Visitors* was given on television there were approximately 12,000,000 viewers. Fourteen radio stations across the country, anchored by WQXR in New York, WFLN in Philadelphia, WGMS in Washington, D. C., WEW in St. Louis, WEAW in Chicago, KIXL in Dallas, KEAR in San Francisco, and KFAC in Los Angeles, play classical and semiclassical records all day long. They have an arrangement whereby they exchange transcribed music not otherwise available to the public.

An estimated 16,000,000 saw the Hallmark Playhouse TV production of *Hamlet*.

It may be recalled that, at the inception of radio, fear was expressed that people would stop going to concerts if they could hear the same symphonies in their homes without cost. Yet concert-hall box-office receipts are proof that radio has educated a huge audience to good music. There is reason to believe that television, particularly color television, will do the same for art, literature, education, history, and the crafts. Already, able critics and teachers are guiding the uninitiated into these provocative realms. A half-hour's tour through a museum with a TV camera can bring to life a wealth of art and knowledge that could otherwise not be seen in months.

ALL this causes the industrial designer to feel that he fills an important role. He, too, is inspired and influenced by the arts, perhaps even more than the culturally awakened man in the street, for it is his responsibility to walk the tight-rope between art and business, always maintaining his professional balance.

When the industrial designer examines a collection of Chinese art, it doesn't follow that his appreciation of its purity of line, its proportions, its perfect use of material, and its rhythm will dictate his next toaster or sewing-machine design. But he learns from all ages. Art and architecture and artifacts are honest historians. They furnish him a reservoir of inspiration. And he doesn't think it is presumptuous to feel that just as the amphora of Greece and the armor of the Middle Ages typified the culture of their times, so will this epoch be judged in part by the best of the mass production of the day.

The *avant-garde* painter, engineer, architect, or craftsman also exerts an influence on the industrial designer, but in a different way. He gives us courage to try new forms, techniques, and materials. A craftsman making a single clock can afford to experiment. The designer working out a model for a manufacturer who will make 40,000 clocks every day cannot. Because so little is at stake financially for him, the craftsman can explore. If his bowl or textile, chair or spoon, seems acceptable to the public, it helps chart our way in advancing the design of mass-produced merchandise. Therefore, we haunt museum exhibits and those stores which display the most extreme designs in modern objects. We observe how they are accepted, as an indication of how far and how fast we may advance. And I have yet to see a craftsman, the purity of whose product we admire, refuse to release his conception into mass production when approached by a manufacturer. It is good for all of us to have good things reach as many people as possible.

Not long ago I was invited to The Hague by the Dutch government to confer with their manufacturers and designers as to what they could do to make their products more palatable to the American consumer. I was anxious to keep my story simple and confine it to mass merchandising. To over-

86

come the language barrier, I decided to try to express my thinking in pictures. I borrowed a Sears Roebuck catalogue of twenty-five years ago and took one of today's, and had slides made of identical merchandise a quarter century apart. I used two large screens and simultaneously projected *before* and *after* shots of dozens of products—household utilities, clothing, farm implements, furniture. I could speak no Dutch, many of the manufacturers could understand no English, but here was an international language. Sears Roebuck is well known in Europe, just as it is in this country, as a giant of merchandisers, and the comparison had great impact. Here was proof, not on a high esoteric level, but on the ground floor of one of the world's largest retailers, that the rise in the level of public taste in America has been phenomenal in the last twenty-five years.

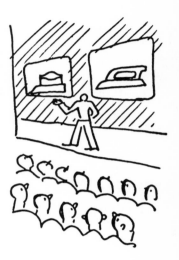

Evidence of this revolution in taste is all about us, in the dime store, in houses, in appliances, transportation, office equipment, hospitals, school buildings, heavy-duty machinery, and farm implements.

Most people have inherent good taste, but they can't be expected to use it if they can't find good things. Many persons are intimidated by what the stores and advertisements tell them is the *proper* thing. Many want what their neighbors have. But given an opportunity to have fine things, people generally choose them. As a result, the American home and office have become standards of good taste throughout the world. To get back to our hypothetical European who loves opera and art and disapproves of our so-called gadget economy, there's probably more bad taste in the form of ugly furniture and hideous decoration in London and Rome than in Pittsburgh and Detroit. But this, too, is changing. As more products of American design find their way into the shops and homes of Europe, or are imitated by European manufacturers, the same metamorphosis will occur there as has taken place here. At last we are repaying the debt of culture to the Old World with well-designed, mass-produced goods. Someday, the housewives of the world may join American women in keeping house with less physical effort—surrounded by objects that will sharpen their over-all taste.

Who can say that the lengthening of the life span of the average American is not owing in part to the contributions of the applied arts? Or that better health may not be attributed partly to lessened fatigue and freedom from concern and toil with old-fashioned methods of work in the home?

This same unshackling has taken place in factories and offices. The job of making a living is easier, safer, more efficient, and pleasanter than it was a quarter century ago. The applied arts have made it possible for average people not only to surround themselves with orderliness and beauty, but to organize their lives so they have more leisure to devote to other things.

It would be fatuous to assume that every man is constantly aware of the details of his surroundings. I do not believe this to be true. But I am convinced that a well-set dinner table will aid the flow of gastric juices; that a well-lighted and planned classroom is conducive to study; that carefully selected colors chosen with an eye to psychological influence will develop better and more lucrative work habits for the man at the machine; that a quietly designed conference room at the United Nations headquarters might well help influence the representatives to make a calm and just decision.

I believe that man achieves his tallest measure of serenity when surrounded by beauty. We find our most serene moments in great cathedrals, in the presence of fine pictures and sculpture, on a university campus, or listening to magnificent music. Industry, technology, and mass production have made it possible for the average man to surround himself with this serenity in his home and in his place of work. Perhaps it is this serenity which we need most in the world today.

CHAPTER 7.

OF ALL the magic of modern civilization, the telephone seems to me the most wondrous achievement. How easily we take for granted that the simple, commonplace spinning of a dial will enable us to talk privately and intimately with a particular person across a city or a continent or an ocean or on a speeding train or a ship at sea or in an auto or a plane several miles in the sky. We assume that the telephone will be there, within reach, in time of stress, to reassure one's family and friends or to transact business.

This assumption is not necessarily an expression of smugness or a feeling that our society is especially endowed, but rather a testimonial to the wonderful democracy of the telephone. It is available alike to millionaire and reliefer. It can be found in stock exchange and boudoir, in saloon and hospital. It has permeated our daily activity and become a personal thing, like reading a letter, and a habit, like brushing the teeth. A child uses it before he learns to read. People unhesitatingly call Washington, New York, Paris, or London.

Other scientific and engineering feats may be more spectacular—the Golden Gate bridge, the Mt. Palomar telescope, this country's fantastic radar screen, the supersonic

90

THE TELEPHONE

jet bomber—but they are things apart. People do not live by them as they do by the ubiquitous telephone.

RECENTLY my plane was delayed for several hours by bad weather on a transcontinental trip, and as soon as it landed I rushed to a phone to relieve any anxiety my wife might have had. She calmly told me she knew the plane was going to be late. She had been on the telephone constantly, and the airline people had kept her informed of weather conditions and the progress of the plane. The incident recalled the "widow's walk" of New England. These were flat areas, with a railing, perched on the gabled roofs of old houses in fishing villages such as Nantucket. During storms, worried seafarers' wives paced these walks, looking out to sea for a glimpse of their husbands' ships returning to port. In a sense, the telephone is a kind of modern "widow's walk." A recent check disclosed that an average of 71,000 telephone inquiries about the weather are made daily in New York City. When storms threatened, the calls sometimes reached 270,000.

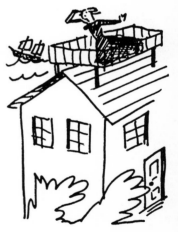

There are now more than 50,000,000 telephones in operation in the United States. Of this number, the Bell System provides service on 41,350,000. The rest are served by independent operating companies substantially all of which have interconnecting facilities with the Bell System. The average subscriber makes 5.5 calls daily—a total of 275,000,000 calls every twenty-four hours. The average length of each conversation is 5.35 minutes, which means that Americans spend 1,471,000,000 minutes or 24,500,000 hours on the telephone every day. For a busy people, this certainly seems excessive. It is difficult to imagine that there can be that much of importance to talk about. Certainly, here is proof that Americans like to talk about little things as well as big things. Here also is an indication of the responsibility the telephone company feels in giving its subscribers an efficient telephone.

Before industrial design as we know it today was appreciated in most businesses, the telephone people had recognized that utility alone was not enough. In 1930, shortly after I opened my office, a representative of the Bell Telephone Laboratories called on me. He graciously displayed no uneasiness over my office furniture—a borrowed card table and folding chairs—all I could afford at the time. His mission was to inform me that the Bell Laboratories were offering thousand-dollar awards to each of ten artists and craftsmen for their conceptions of the future appearance of the telephone.

It was flattering to be included in such a group, and the prospect of a thousand dollars was attractive. But I suggested that a telephone's appearance should be developed from the inside out, not merely created as a mold into which the engineers would eventually squeeze the mechanism, and this would require collaboration with Bell technicians. My visitor disagreed, saying such collaboration would only limit a designer's artistic scope.

Several months later he returned with a changed point of view. He admitted frankly that the telephones of the future submitted by the ten commissioned artists had been unsatisfactory. Some of them were quite original, he said, but all of them were impractical. Now he wanted to hear my ideas about design from the inside out. Our conversation led to an association that has proved eminently satisfying. No one could have been more co-operative than the Bell engineers have been through the years, or so patient and understanding.

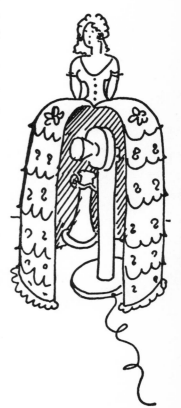

Today the convenience of telephones is established, and they occupy the most accessible place in the home or office or store. Twenty-five years ago some people weren't quite sure where to put them. They were sometimes kept inside plaster globes of the world or cabinets or dolls with fluffy skirts. Because placement had a bearing on design, we had to determine what people did with phones, and that is why the telephone company permitted me to act as a repairman's helper when he went on his rounds. My research ended abruptly when I went up in the service elevator of an apartment house and was ushered through the kitchen into the living quarters of a family I knew. There my hostess of a previous evening greeted me in some confusion and seemed surprised that a man who had represented himself as an industrial designer should be repairing telephones.

The telephone for which the Bell people were seeking a new appearance combined several features. After long development, the most serious operating faults of the so-

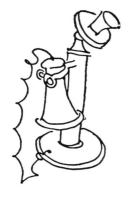

called "French" phone or handset had been overcome. The resulting combination of a handset with parts of the old stand-up phone had produced the early cradle-type instrument. The proposed design, with smaller components housed within the instrument, would eliminate the box on the wall that held the ringing apparatus. In the final design, plastic was substituted for the metal housing. This is the type of phone in general use today.

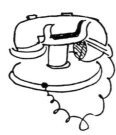

Eight years ago the Bell people again began to discuss with us their ideas for another new telephone instrument. They wanted improved sound, volume, comfort, dial mechanism, new materials—in short, a new design. This was the beginning of what became the 500-Type Telephone Set—the instrument now being installed all over the country—and the start of another long collaboration between the Bell engineering staff and our office, involving a mountainous file of data and incalculable testing.

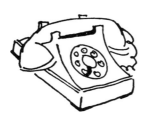

In seeking a new telephone appearance, the Bell people were confronted with a consideration in which the user was not primarily involved. The form had to be classic so that it would not be out of place with shorter-lived objects in homes and offices either at the time of introduction or twenty years later, the estimated life span of the instrument.

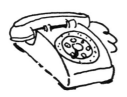

THIS is a good place to point out that designing a telephone is not quite the same as designing a clock or a vacuum cleaner or a radio. In the accepted sense, there is no consumer sales problem. Telephone subscribers do not buy their telephones; they use the instruments the Bell system makes available to them because telephones are part of the

94

integrated over-all service that they purchase from the telephone company. Yet salesmanship of the highest order is still involved. The Bell System owes much of its growth to its acute awareness of public relations and its alertness to the subtleties in the relationship of men and machines. The telephone people want each piece of equipment to be an ambassador of good will. They know the subscriber will be pleased, perhaps subconsciously, when he finds the handset grip is more comfortable than the old model and that the voices of his friends are transmitted more clearly.

Toward this goal, we proceed slowly, discarding more innovations than we accept. We have to consider that phones are used not only on desks and tables while people are sitting, but also on counters and shelves for stand-up use. We have to give critical consideration to room lighting and to arm, wrist, and finger angles and motion in the dial operation.

Maintenance, always a factor in a new design, did not present too great a problem in the 500-Type set, as the maintenance record of the old instrument had been excellent. Nevertheless, to permit a greater degree of accessibility for repair, etc., Bell engineers fastened all components to the base plate. Previously, some of the components had been fastened inside the cover and others on the base plate.

The handset was re-engineered by the Bell people for better performance. Data in Bell files on the measurement of two thousand faces, to determine the average spacing between mouth and ear, were re-examined and interpreted in terms of a new instrument. Every conceivable kind of hand-grip was considered—triangular in cross section like its predecessor, square, a thin rectangle, a thick rectangle, and many mongrel forms. The final selection was the thick rectangle, slimmed down. In comparison with its predecessor, it was smaller, lighter, more comfortable, resisted turning in the hand, and looked better.

Drawing on years of experience with the dial number plate used on coin collectors in public telephone booths, Bell engineers expanded the existing three-inch dial of the desk telephone set to four and one quarter inches, the letters and numbers were placed outside the finger wheel, and the white characters were molded in black. (In the old dial, black letters and red numbers were printed on white under the wheel.) With the new placement, dragging fingers and pencils could no longer deface the characters, the flickering effect of the spinning wheel was eliminated, the characters could be made larger, the dial was easier to clean. Laboratory and field tests by typical telephone users under typical dialing conditions have pointed up these advantages.

Once Bell engineers established the basic position for the handset and dial, the phone began to fall into shape. This is an easy way of stating that something like 2500 rough sketches were scrutinized and narrowed down to half a dozen. Curiously enough, the first form conceived for the new combined set was generically the same as the form finally accepted.

IT WOULD serve no purpose to confound the reader with the infinite mass of statistical detail that had to be carefully studied, the suggested changes that were agreed upon, rejected, or modified, and the compromises effected between engineers and industrial designer. Inherent limitations dictated much of the design. The bell, for instance, had to be placed at the rear because, as the largest component, this was the only area available.

Our office was in turmoil for weeks over what was called the "ROH Battle"—receiver off hook. The telephone company has a pronounced distaste for hang-up errors—the subscriber should properly replace the handset on the cradle, so that the plunger buttons do not remain up, thus keeping the line closed and unavailable for subsequent calls —and lengthy discussions were held over whether two or four prongs on the cradle lessened this possibility.

Early designs of the new housing were unsatisfactory on two counts. They were too high, appearing taller than the old model, and the cradle prongs took away the sleek appearance that was desired. After renewed analysis, Bell engineers found that the housing could be lowered an important one eighth of an inch. Our contribution was optical. By making small changes in the shape of the housing, the position of the light reflection was changed, thus making the instrument *look* even lower.

Sketches were made of all these variations, then accurate layout drawings. These were followed by full-size "bread-board models" of the components. When several designs appeared likely, they were modeled in clay, which can easily be modified as ideas develop. Later they were cast in plaster, sculptured and lacquered. This high polish was important so that the model could be analyzed for light reflection that might prove annoying or tiring. Some were equipped with mock components such as handset dials,

97

cords, and number plates to simulate the finished product. When all decisions were made, a bronze master was made of the final design. From this, the finished housing evolved, made of cellulose acetate butyrate.

The task has not ended there. The telephone family is a large one. Commercially, not only telephone sets are involved, but also switchboard facilities and related installations. The new design also made allowance for special types of telephones—hard-of-hearing sets, four- and six-button sets, and two-line single-button sets, to permit interoffice communication and extended service. Some of these functions can be incorporated into the standard housing design, but special variations will require modifications.

It can be mentioned that our work with Bell also goes beyond civilian applications. Modified versions of telephone equipment and special detection and communication devices have been developed for the armed services. The Bell Laboratories engineer such devices as radar on the mast of a battleship or sonar equipment in a submarine. Since World War II our office has participated with Bell on 114 projects of diversified nature. But the appearance of the new 500-Type Telephone Set, like that of its predecessor, is the symbol of our relationship.

In recognition of the increasing use of color in the decorative schemes of homes and offices, the 500 Set has been made available in a range of colors, although the familiar black will long be with us.

THE NEW telephone is already in many homes and offices, and the Bell people and our staff are very proud of it.

98

It represents eight years of heartening and rewarding co-operation between Bell administrative, engineering, research, and sales personnel and our office. It is a tangible monument to integration. The lesson we all learned in contributing to a new and better telephone instrument was that all parts of an old design need not be changed for the sake of change, that some parts have proved themselves through years of use but that better devices, techniques, and materials may justify a change. One of these is the bell, which has a four-position volume-control wheel under the base plate, permitting users to select the bell volume they prefer.

The telephone has become a compelling force in modern society, to the point that people's lives are actually geared to it. Inevitably, a few persons complain that it intrudes on their privacy. There is a compulsion to answer a ringing telephone, even though it may break into a business conference or an intimate conversation with a friend. But automobile horns, church bells, airplanes flying overhead—and a baby's cry at midnight—are distractions, too, and they are equally purposeful. Fortunately, so far as the telephone is concerned, what used to be a delicate problem in etiquette has come to be so well understood that offense is rarely taken.

It is inescapable that a sense of urgency be attached to a ringing telephone. It may be merely someone calling to accept an invitation to a birthday party, but it may also be an emergency that could affect lives. Perhaps it is wise to consider a telephone call in its proper perspective. It is relatively meaningless when a sixth-grade student calls a chum, and they do their homework jointly over the phone. But it may affect the future of the world when a president calls a prime minister.

CHAPTER 8.

SOMEDAY, perhaps, everyone will have his own magic carpet, powered by the smashed atom, and glide noiselessly to and from work and on week-end picnics with the family.

Meanwhile, by comparison with the uncomfortable, depressing, and claustrophobic public transportation of a quarter century ago, the traveler isn't doing too badly.

Under normal circumstances a man setting out on a journey may confidently expect as much comfort and service as, or perhaps more than, he is accustomed to in his home.

If he's in a hurry, he will take a plane. If he has more time, he will take a train or a ship. If expense is a problem or it's a short trip, he will take a bus. In any case, whether hurtling through space at four hundred miles an hour or doing a steady fifty on Highway 66, he need not anticipate a grueling, tiring ride. He can look forward to a pleasant trip and to arriving at his destination reasonably relaxed and refreshed. A vast change has occurred in public transportation in the last twenty-five years. As a result, travel is nearer the dream of the effortless magic carpet than it was in the day of the jolting stagecoach.

LAND, SEA, AND AIR

THE industrial designer's work in public carriers is a departure from his contributions to mass-produced articles. Whereas vacuum cleaners, stoves, and thermostats are machine-manufactured in vast quantities and made available in the market, a train, a ship, or a plane is custom-designed. However, it is used by a mass public, and the industrial designer's techniques and understanding of the mass mind can be readily applied to transportation.

Here the designer's problem, briefly, is to create comfortable living space inside a moving vehicle. To achieve it, he must think in terms of the vehicle's size, its speed, the length of its trip, its capacity, and how much luxury is desired. A train runs on a fixed roadbed and its movement is predictable, therefore loose furniture and accessories can be used. In a ship or plane or bus, which is subject to sudden, unforeseen movement, things have to be fastened down. The airplane gives great speed over long distances and rapid service between points where land traffic is heavy. The railroad car is similar to the bus and plane in that it is in the shape of a long, narrow corridor, but, unlike them, there is no need to cram every function into one unit. These functions can be spread out because cars are assembled in trains. In a ship, with its greater spaciousness, a different set of values prevails. But in all these the determining factor is cost—how, through design, can the operator of a transportation line supply the most speed and comfort at the least cost to the traveler and still make a profit?

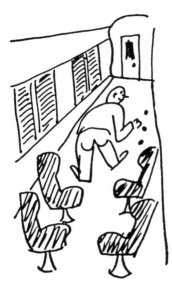

Someone once remarked that George Pullman walked through a railroad car and planted seeds in even rows and the regimented chairs and tables that sprouted were the result. Certainly, the railroads resisted change for a long time. Until the industrial designer was called in, car interiors were not only uncomfortable, but were a fearful display of bad taste.

When wooden cars were replaced by steel cars, the railroads had an opportunity to make changes for the better. But they went ahead, imitating the discarded mahogany interior with a painted reproduction of wood graining on metal. All carpets and upholstery, for some reason, had to be a bilious green. Lighting more often than not was in the shape of candelabra, and wall brackets with electric bulbs were in the inefficient form of candle flames. The American public was forced to sleep on shelves reminiscent of an opium den, imprisoned behind dirt-catching green curtains. Some few trains still have open-berth cars, but the trend has been to liberate the traveler from these atrocities.

The ideal in train design is a car-to-car integration of all passenger comforts. Operationally this can be difficult to accomplish because the volume of traffic fluctuates. The need for removing or adding cars constantly upsets the make-up of a train.

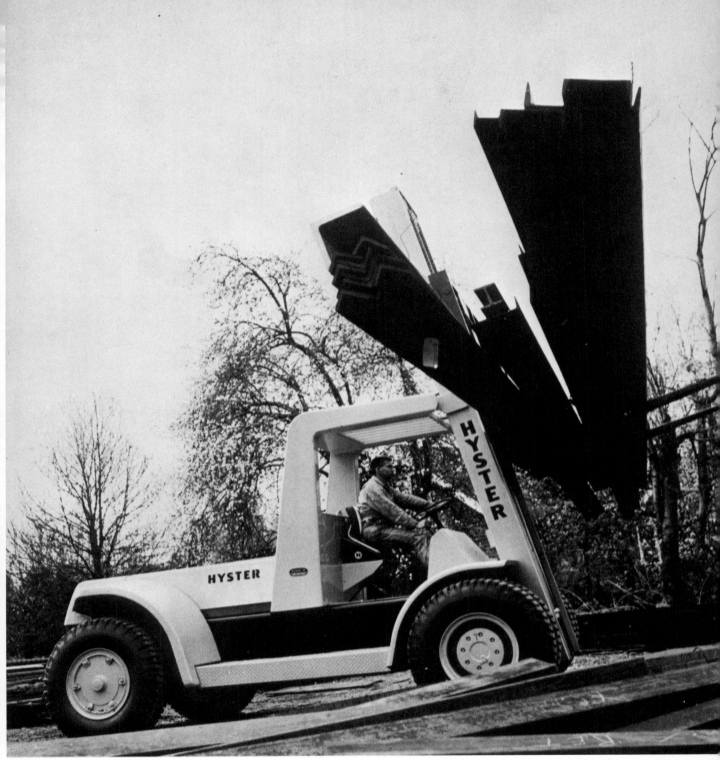

When you have to lift or lower or push or pull a heavy load, you don't want any frills. Hyster material-moving and road construction machines must be simple, strong and stable. And they must look it. Above is a lift truck capable of handling a 22,500 pound load.

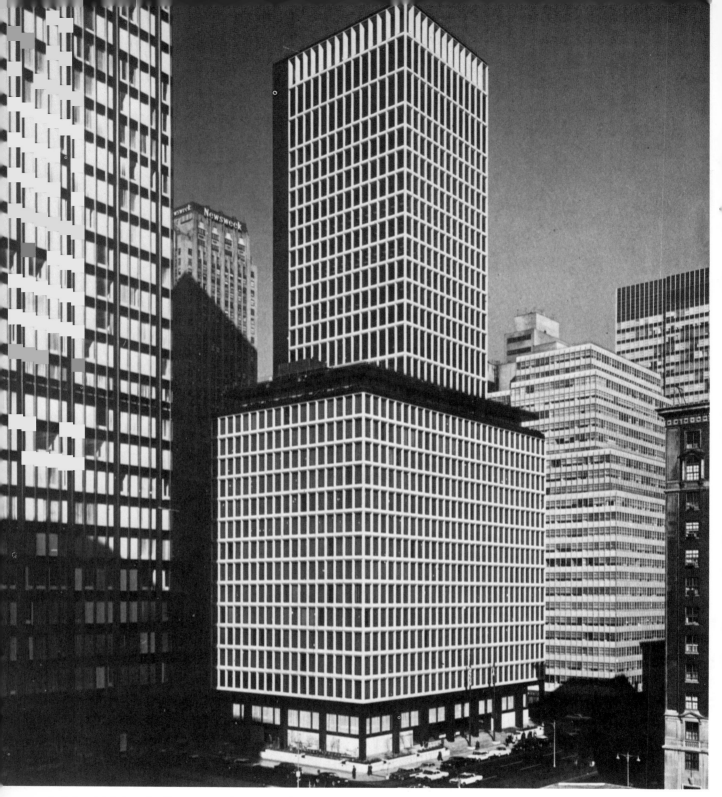

An industrial designer hardly ever gets a chance to turn his experience and imagination loose on a whole office building—inside and out— from architecture to ashtrays. But the Bankers Trust Company wanted its Park Avenue headquarters in New York to have a unity of feeling, and decided this could best be attained by having one designer conceive and control the total project.

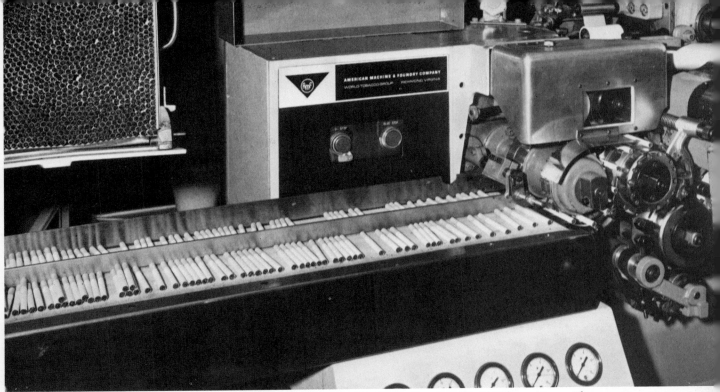

Above is one of a line of equipment manufactured by American Machine & Foundry's World Tobacco Group. This apparatus automatically attaches filter tips to cigarettes.

AMFare, shown below, is American Machine & Foundry's version of automated cooking. Everyone likes to eat—especially when no one has to cook! Food is ordered over a microphone; buttons on a console start the machines; hamburgers, shrimp, chicken, fish, french fries, or what you will—each responds to the order.

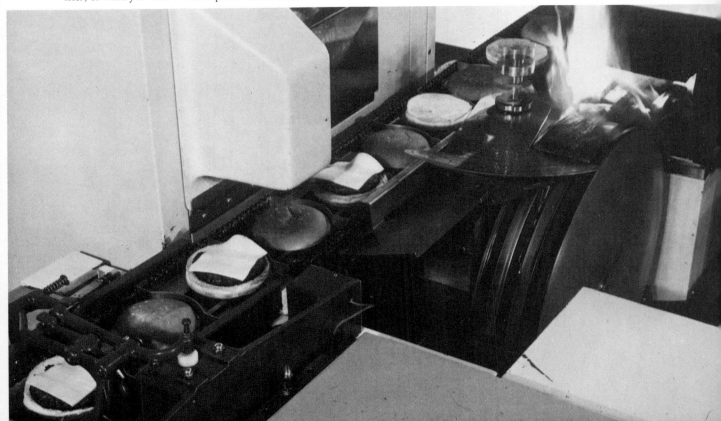

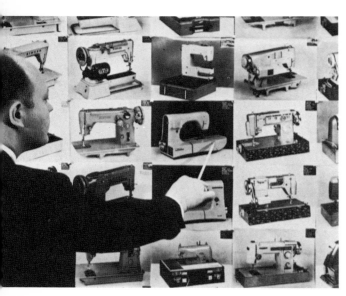

1 We start by studying the competition. We analyze models and illustrations of other companies' merchandise, both here and from abroad.

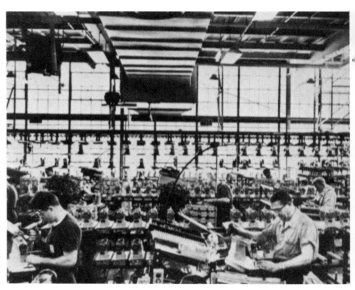

2 We familiarize ourselves with the client's manufacturing facilities. We like to know the limitations as well as the potentials of his plants.

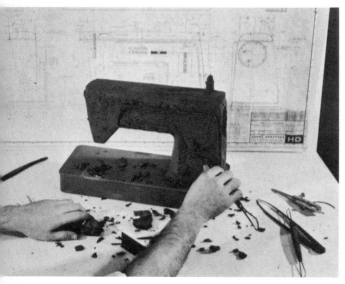

5 Now we're ready to study the design in three dimensions. We start this phase of the work with a rough clay model.

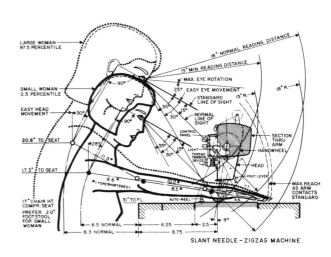

6 Using the anthropometric techniques we originated, we turn to human engineering. We see how a mother and daughter will use the machine.

The distance between drawing board and assembly line is not one inspired leap for the industrial designer but rather a series of careful and patient steps. Our development of Singer's Model 600 sewing machine is typical. Although there is an infinity of steps in between, the eight shown here are fundamental to our approach to a client's problem.

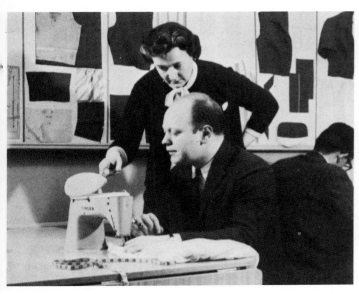

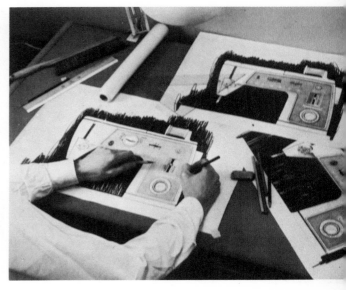

3 We learn how the product will be used. In developing Model 600, our designers took a Singer sewing course, Singer zig-zag stitching and all.

4 After consultations with top management, sales executives and engineers, we develop a variety of idea sketches.

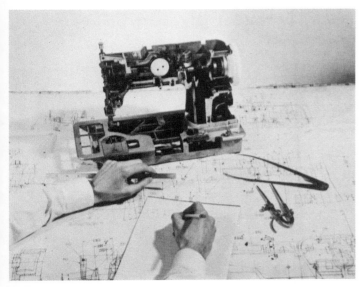

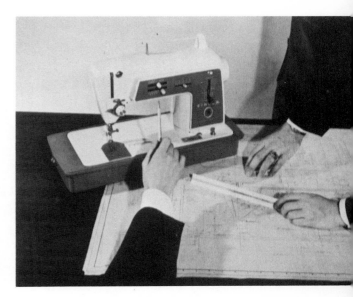

7 Through each step there is close collaboration with our client's engineers. Working drawings are made and checked against their pilot model.

8 A prototype model—identical to the production-line product in every detail—completes the project. Exit designer. Enter sales team.

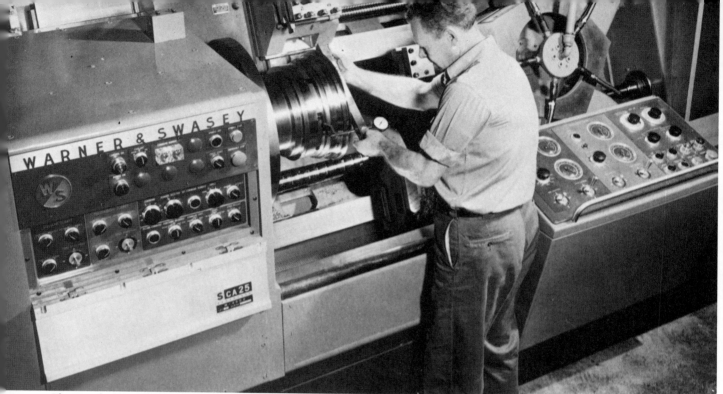

The Servofeed is an automated turret lathe made by Warner & Swasey. It goes on and on, making parts of other machines, all at the bidding of a properly-programmed tape. The industrial designer's focus was on safety, maintenance and giving the machine an appearance that expressed its utility and its excellence.

AMF's Bowling Products Group "Streamlane 21" is responsible for the world wide popularity of the ancient sport of bowling. Today the alleys are completely automated, from the ball return to the mechanical pin setter. "Streamlane 21" shown here is formed of extra large moldings of thermoplastic.

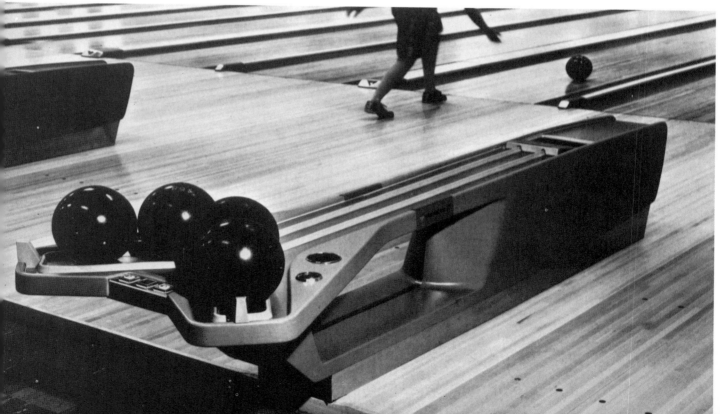

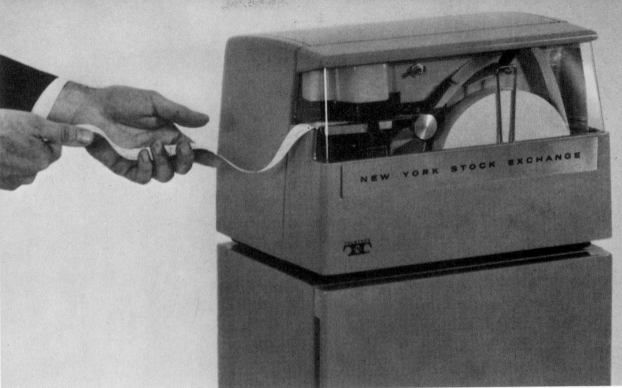

No one likes to wait for the stock ticker. The Teletype Corporation produced this apparatus to handle nine hundred characters a minute—80% faster than the machine it replaced. Visibility and easy access to the tape and printing mechanism are important.

The high speed Teletypewriter shown below sends or receives messages instantaneously over the telephone wires, to and from any point on earth. Its base contains intricate electronic components and the small desk top unit beside it houses the call control facilities.

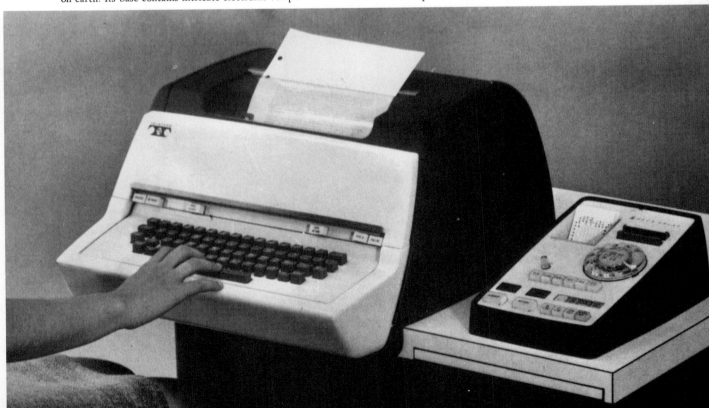

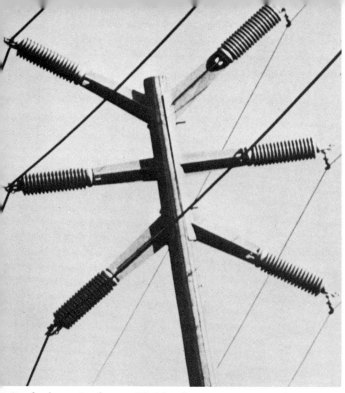

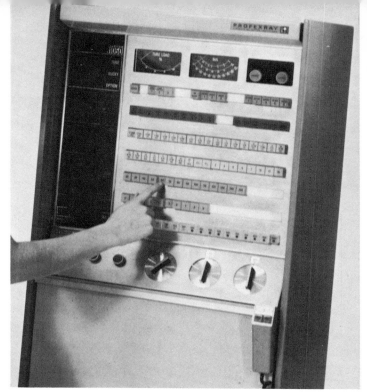

Our landscape is often modified by the common power pole. Southern California Edison Co. wanted a pole to present a simple, harmonious, unobtrusive silhouette.

Controls, often used in an emergency, must be obvious and sequential. This 900 milliampere x-ray generator is a component of Litton Industries Profexray line of equipment that looks through Joe and Josephine.

This sculptured form is American Safety Razor's stainless steel razor. Pragmatic as shaving itself, its sleekness allows the clean sweep that means a clean shave.

Telautograph's Facsimile-transmitter is simple to operate. It sends pictures, maps or letters via telephone lines between plants, cities or continents.

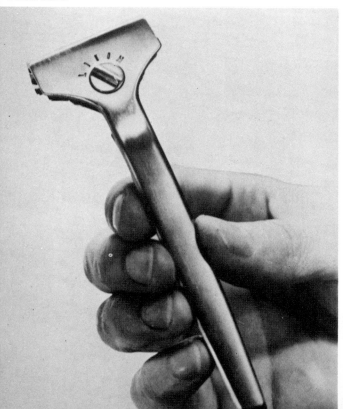

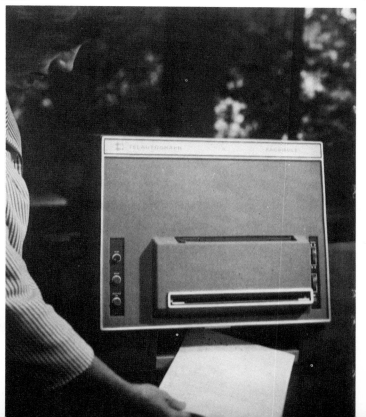

As any housewife knows, the most difficult space to make attractive is a long and narrow corridor. Nevertheless, the industrial designer has successfully arranged corridorlike trains to appear as a series of comfortable, well-proportioned rooms. Contrasting colors have been introduced to create the feeling of space, and chairs and private rooms now assure relaxation.

For years observation cars had the furniture arranged with passengers' backs to the windows. Now the seats are placed so that the traveler faces large windows and can actually observe the passing landscape without getting a crick in his neck.

In our work on railroad cars for the New York Central, we set out to create the atmosphere and character of a fine club in the diners and lounge cars. This was done by installing the type of furniture, the colors, and the materials expected in a club, but retaining, architecturally, the clean lines possible in a modern railroad car. We broke up the long passageways by placing divans and tables crosswise. This technique was notably successful in the Twentieth Century Limited. We also used restful beiges or earthy tones, with bright colors as harmonious accents. Occasionally we used mirrors to give the feeling of width. As if by magic, the cars no longer had the appearance of a well-tilled cabbage field.

The interiors were purposely kept simple, with no extraneous detail. We have learned to visualize an interior of a public conveyance as a background that will sometimes be crowded, sometimes be half full, occasionally have only one or two persons in it, never be empty. These people will

111

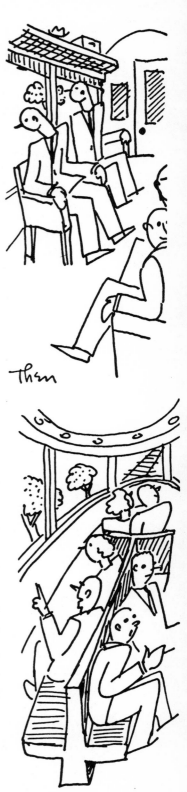

Then

Now

be wearing different kinds of clothing, depending on the season and the time of day. Their clothes will be of various colors. Many of them will be reading bright-colored magazines or books. We use decorated panels and murals sparingly because the presence of people makes the interior sufficiently "busy." In addition, we consider these people in terms of acoustics. When every seat is taken, they add a great deal of sound-absorbing "upholstery."

Train exteriors acquired the new look they have today in the early thirties and haven't been changed much since. Railroad men found that ease of maintenance was more important than fancy skirts and pseudo streamlining, which had a brief flair, and settled on standardized cars.

In railroad-car design, as in other things, trial and error can be the best guide. On the first trains our office did, the fleet of Mercurys that run from Cleveland, Detroit, and Chicago, we specified the installation of an electric eye on the door between the galley and the dining car. At first the mysteriously opening door frightened the waiters and some of them dropped their trays, but they soon became accustomed to it and learned to appreciate its convenience.

Oddly enough, the Mercurys almost died aborning. The final designs were approved by the late Fred Williamson, president of the New York Central System, but when they were put out for bid the prices were so out of line that the project was canceled. It was a heavy blow when I received the bad news, for the trains had been a major effort for our office. I decided to take the rest of the day off, and I boarded a train for the country. En route, traveling through the railroad yards at Mott Haven, I saw the answer. I got off the train, returned to New York, and suggested to President Williamson that some of the unused cars in the yards might be converted. Out of them the successful Mercurys were built at one quarter the original figure. The Mercurys have been called a turning point in railroad design. They were the first streamliners done as a unit, inside and out, integrating everything from locomotives to dinner china.

When the first Mercury neared completion in the New York Central's Indianapolis shops, I made a routine inspection of the project. My visit coincided with that of one of the railroad's vice-presidents, a man who wore high button shoes and vigorously opposed change. He walked through the train from locomotive to observation car, glancing fiercely at my handiwork and making no attempt to conceal his dislike. I followed in meek silence. At the end of his tour he said nothing, so I asked what he thought of it. "Cleopatra's barge!" he snorted, and walked away.

When Edward Bernays, the public-relations expert, took his first trip on a Mercury he wired me, "You have made gentlemen out of traveling salesmen." He meant no slight to a noble segment of business life. He was referring to our elimination of the traditional spittoon. It is true that many persons leave their manners at home when they travel. They place their feet on walls and furniture and deface clean surfaces. The point here is that the absence of the spittoons went unnoticed, bearing out my belief that people reflect the environment and atmosphere in which they are placed. Well-designed and maintained equipment psychologically reduces misuse.

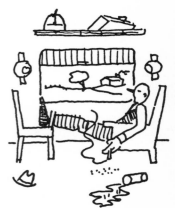

We have often been asked why the vista dome used by

the Western railroads was not included on the Twentieth Century Limited. The question carries a hint that we were behind the times. Many years ago we had designed a glass-enclosed structure protruding from the roof of an observation car—in fact, we were prepared to release the drawings for it to the railroad. One evening, while rushing through New York's Grand Central Station, I was struck with a disturbing thought. I let my Chicago-bound train leave without me. Instead I checked some measurements we should have checked previously. My suspicion proved correct. Our vista dome would have been sliced off on its first trip as it came to the low Park Avenue tunnel that all trains pass through to enter the station.

I have learned to be on my guard when traveling on trains or ships or planes our office has designed, because of the well-meaning people who have suggestions, usually impractical, for added fillips here and there. But there's always the possibility they may really suggest an improvement we have overlooked. One morning during the initial run of the Twentieth Century Limited there was a knock on my compartment door. I was expecting the porter with my suit, sent out the night before to be pressed, but it was a large maid, who asked, "Are you Mr. Dreyfuss, who designed this train?" She continued, "Did you design my uniform?" I said our office had supervised it, and asked what was wrong with it. She said scornfully, "It looks mammy-made." I have always treasured the expression. When we got to Chicago I took her to Marshall Field's and bought her a uniform she thought was more appropriate to the new train—"something in gray moire with a zipper."

ONE day John E. Slater, president of American Export Lines, asked me to lunch at his club in New York. As coffee was served, he said, "I'm going to write a question that I don't want anyone to hear." He took an envelope from his pocket, scribbled on the back of it, and pushed it across the table. I read, "Do you have the time to do the interiors for some transatlantic liners?" I looked at him, saw he was in earnest, and wrote, "Yes" under his question. This envelope was our only contract during the first months of our long association.

We started the next day on the largest job our office had ever undertaken. The ships turned out to be the *Independence* and the *Constitution*. Each was to cost approximately $25,000,000, have thousand-passenger capacity in three classes and a crew of five hundred, a 29,500 tonnage, a 683-foot over-all length, a speed in excess of twenty-six knots.

Our first concern was planning staterooms, public rooms, and public spaces. We worked with Bethlehem's Central Technical Division at Quincy, Massachusetts, and I am afraid we gave them a great deal of apprehension. Our ignorance of sacred cows of ship joinery and lack of respect for tradition brought out a number of unorthodox ideas, which shocked the industry. One was our insistence that bulkheads be constructed without the busy effect created by moldings or batten strips at the joints. As a result, I became known as Henry "No Batten" Dreyfuss. A satisfactory scheme for construction without battens was finally worked out by using a frankly undisguised V-joint.

When our drawings were about two thirds completed, we suddenly were confronted with disappointment, just as we had been previously in planning the Mercurys. In this case, a disagreement arose between the owners and the government, and the project was temporarily abandoned.

At this point American Export decided to buy and reconvert four Exporter-class vessels that had served as attack transports during the war, to replace their Four Aces, three of which had been sunk in action in Navy service. These new Aces carried 125 passengers, were about 10,000 tons and 473 feet long. Like their ill-fated predecessors, they were called the *Excalibur, Exeter, Excambian,* and *Exochorda.*

The concept we had developed for the larger ships was put to use, with modification, on these new Aces, with the thought that they might be somewhat of an experimental laboratory should work resume on the *Independence* and *Constitution.* This is exactly what happened. Shortly before the Aces were completed, work was resumed on the big ships.

In such a gigantic project, close liaison was mandatory, and as the work swung into high gear, a fine pattern of cooperation was established. Meetings were held about once a week with representatives of the Maritime Administration, of Bethlehem, the joinery contractor, and the industrial designer. These meetings were not always peaceful, but they were friendly. Meanwhile, American Export had set up two committees, one headed by John Slater and made up of department heads, and a second composed of representatives of all departments. This second committee discussed and voted on all matters of design and arrangement, approved materials and the hundreds of items that go into a ship. If the vote on a recommendation was not unanimous it was referred to the higher group.

Our staff consisted of a project manager and an assistant, a chief designer, an architect, a decorator, and a considerable number of draftsmen. In addition, consultants were called in on art selection, lighting, and acoustics. Tens of thousands of drawings and sketches were made. Quarter-inch scale models of all the public rooms and their furnishings were constructed. These were first used to give Export a graphic exhibit of what we were doing, then for publicity purposes, and finally used by the shipyard foremen to aid in visualizing the designs. We checked countless shop drawings made by the shipyard and the joinery contractor.

All the furniture was designed by our office. Personal experience—a conked shin sustained on a sea voyage years before—caused me to insist on all exposed corners being rounded. The furniture was kept small in scale to counteract low headroom and small rooms, and it was arranged to break up the usable space into small areas so that a "hotel-lobby feeling" might be avoided. Mirrors and pictures emphasizing depth and perspective were used to give the air-conditioned inside staterooms an atmosphere of spaciousness and livability comparable to the outside rooms, which had portholes.

When the time came to select artists to do the murals in the public rooms, we visited many artists and galleries, determined to put the art appropriation of more than $100,000 per ship to the best possible use. We wanted outstanding art that was not extreme in either direction. When the final choices were made and approved by the Maritime Administration, the work went ahead with no displays of temperament. In fact, when an uncaught error in construction forced one artist to crop his finished mural a foot, he did so without complaints. A sculptress, however, became so fond of the decorative effect of her signature that it appeared in finished form in large red letters. Furthermore, she rejected all suggestions that it be reduced. Fortunately, the other side of the figure was equally beautiful, and when the front was turned to face a bulkhead, no one except the sculptress noticed the difference.

Probably no other industrial designer was ever given such complete control as we were on these ships. Even the china and the glassware and much of the silver were made from our designs. Each ship was equipped with 16,800 pieces of china, more than 6600 pieces of hollow ware, 7720 pieces of flat silver. More than 6350 yards of fabrics were furnished by twenty-eight different firms, and five carpetmakers supplied eight thousand yards of carpeting per ship. We designed sugar and soap wrappers, menus, writing paper, cards, paper napkins, matches, ash trays, directional signs, flower vases, and the stewards' uniforms.

Seven years after my luncheon with John Slater I was among several hundred guests invited to go by special train from New York to Boston the day the *Independence* was to sail from the Quincy shipyards and ride back for the gala reception New York Harbor gives new liners. At the last moment I canceled my train reservation and took a plane. I wanted to walk on that finished ship alone, before the hundreds of well-wishers arrived. When I walked up the gangplank, the great ship seemed almost deserted. But as I looked the length of its deck, I saw a solitary figure approaching and I recognized John Slater. He, too, had felt the urge to be alone with his completed dream. We walked around the ship together, and very little was said, although I am sure we were both thinking of what that simple question on the back of an envelope years before had wrought. As we completed the inspection, he said, "I wouldn't change a single thing."

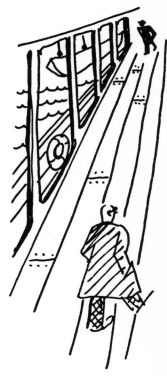

I PAID my first airplane fare twenty-five years ago for a flight in a single-engined plane from Chicago to Springfield, Illinois. I was the only passenger, and there were no seats. I sat on the mailbags.

My first transcontinental flight was in a Ford three-engined plane with wicker chairs. The trip took three days, and we spent each night in hotels on the ground. By comparison with today's swift, comfortable air travel, it seems primitive.

Yet the day is nearing when jet transports will span the Atlantic or America in three hours. It will be a race against the sun, and, allowing for the time change, a person will arrive in Los Angeles the moment he leaves New York.

This new era can be contemplated only with awe and respect for the engineers who have mastered the science of aerodynamics. But it is well to remember that whatever the speed, certain fixed economic conditions prevail in commercial aviation. To provide regular, reliable service at rates people can afford, and make a profit, the air lines must utilize every ounce of weight, every inch of space.

These two restrictions, weight and space, are riveted into the mind of everyone who works on a plane. When Robert Gross, president of the Lockheed Aircraft Corporation, engaged our office to design the interiors for the new Super Constellation, we found ourselves thinking in terms of ounces. A cost breakdown showed that every pound of weight we could save meant $2065 in added revenue over the estimated fifteen-year life of the plane. Thus, items that might increase passenger comfort must frequently be sacrificed because they are too heavy or too big. There are ways, however, of tastefully planning an interior within the prescribed limits. Lightweight carpeting can be used, dark-colored fabrics that give a feeling of solidarity, and Fiberglas for the stuffing of chairs and mattresses and thin rather than thick leather and honeycomb panels for partitions.

Fundamentally, the designer is presented by the airplane manufacturer with the inside of a huge, inelastic pickle or cigar. Its exterior form, which can vary in size every half inch of the length of the plane, is inexorably set by the laws of aerodynamics. The only thing the designer can squeeze in is his imagination.

At a quick glance, it might seem that an airplane interior is designed from the outside in, which would be contrary to the basic concept of industrial design that the inside machinery of a product should dictate the outside form. Actually, the aerodynamics or outside of the airplane constitutes the "machinery" that causes it to force itself through the air. Therefore, while we design in reverse in this instance, the principle that function should dictate the design remains the same.

One of the ironies of making airplane passengers comfortable is that, although the allotted space is inflexible, the airlines demand complete flexibility. Transport planes must be readily adaptable to any type of use. On long trips they carry fewer passengers than normally because they require more fuel. As a result, transoceanic planes usually have greater seat spacing than others. But they must be easily convertible for close seating on shorter, less expensive trips or completely dismantled inside for emergency use by the armed forces or for hauling freight. Any of these change-overs can be made rapidly because of the tracks installed flush with the floor, the length of the cabin, in most planes. The seats, the bulkheads, even the galley equipment, can be fastened to them so that they are adjustable or removable, should the need arise.

The seat is easily the most important ingredient in the airplane interior. Make a man comfortable, and everything looks rosy to him. He can relax, his food tastes better, the trip will seem hours shorter.

Joe and Josephine have been of inestimable assistance in seat design. We know, too well, that everyone is of slightly different size and proportion, and a seat must accommodate them all. Our charts help, and our consultant orthopedist has added to our knowledge. In this case, we dissented from the advice of doctors that passengers would be less fatigued if harder, spine-supporting seats were used. Psychology is important in flying, and we know that passengers enjoy the luxury and security of sinking into a well-upholstered chair. Today's airplane seat is a compromise.

The airplane seat of tomorrow will be completely adjust-

121

able forward, back, up, and down. By the turn of a knob, the passenger will select his choice of several degrees of softness or firmness. The seat will have a rectractable leg rest. It will have adjustable "ears," like the old fireside chairs, to provide a headrest and a degree of privacy. The left "ear" will have an individual reading light that will not disturb a neighbor. The right "ear" will have a small, personally controlled amplifier for announcements, radio programs, or recorded music. Lights, amplifier—in fact, the whole seating unit will be plugged into a handy outlet as a housewife plugs in her electric toaster. There will be space under or next to each seat for baggage stowage. A call bell for the stewardess will be located in the armrest. Most important, the seat will afford the greatest possible safety in rough air or in an emergency landing.

This seems to be asking a great deal of a poor chair, but actually it's not intended to be a simple chair, any more than is a dentist's or a barber's chair. It will be a complicated piece of machinery that affords safety, comfort, convenience, and privacy. Because it will be self-contained, the seat will be movable, to accommodate heavy or light passenger loads, since it need not be located adjacent to the button and lights now located in the walls of the cabin. The present complication in this shifting is that the chairs will no longer be adjacent to windows. There is a potential solution to this problem. Nowadays, a plane's aluminum skin is vital to its strength. Every window or door cut in this stressed skin reduces its strength and necessitates "beefing up" the supporting structure. One day a transparent metal or a clear plastic with the strength and lightness of titanium may permit a continuous window the length of the fuselage, broken only by the necessary rings of framework. Such an arrangement would permit complete freedom in shifting the chairs and provide visibility at any point.

Inherent in this vision is the suggestion that airplane interiors will look different than they do today. We appear to be in a transitional period. Such earth-bound symbols as upholstered seats and carpets and little window curtains have given this pioneer generation of air travelers a security that was needed. Now that they have that security, passengers may anticipate interiors designed along functional lines. Everything will change except man, the passenger, and with his recently acquired confidence in flight and a maturing psychology, he will be ready to accept an airplane interior that looks and performs like a machine racing through the stratosphere rather than the front parlor it imitates today.

With the jet transport, engineers have made a Flash Gordon dream a reality long before most of us expected it. Industrial designers must now consider new factors and limitations. For example, we have employed every acoustical device to quiet outside engine noises, but supersonic planes will present an eerie silence, and the problem is reversed. The conversation of one hundred passengers in a fuselage could become annoying, requiring the use of sound-absorbing materials. One might well ask, will the quiet of the plane require a general musical background? Or will it demand compartmentations so that those who wish to enjoy that quiet will not be annoyed by passengers who wish recreation?

When we were studying jet transportation for Lockheed, a member of our staff commuted between London and Rome on the British Comets. He was impressed with the plane's remarkable rate and angle of climb and the relatively low noise level for the power and speed involved. He described this noise as more the sound of a rushing wind than the noise of piston-engine aircraft. Cruising at 39,000 feet gave surprisingly little added sensation of height than normal cruising at 18,000. Passengers, this survey reported, appeared to feel that everything about the flight was normal. This survey will enable us to translate his findings into the demands of tomorrow.

Not all the problems of passenger flight occur within the cylinder we call the fuselage. A major complaint from Joe and Josephine is the length of time required to recover luggage at the point of destination. It is annoying to get from New York to Washington in about an hour, then wait twenty minutes for your bag. I once kept a little black book for an entire year, jotting down the time of each flight and, alongside, the time it took to get my bags. At the end of the year I mailed the depressing totals to some of my airline friends.

All kinds of mechanical aids have been devised, and ground crews have been intensively trained to speed the handling of luggage, but not too much progress has been made. Lockheed has developed a gondola-type container into which luggage is stored as it is checked at the airline desk. The gondola is wheeled to the plane and fastened to the underside of the ship, where it remains in flight. The process is reversed at the destination.

124

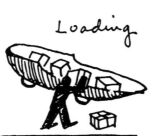

Loading

in flight

I carry a bag of my own design, out of which I can live for three days. It fits under my plane seat. Along with my clothes and toilet articles, it contains a supply of large manila envelopes, stamped and addressed, which I use to mail my laundry home each day. With increased use of synthetic fabrics that can be easily washed and dried and require no ironing, perhaps the ever-increasing flying public will reduce its wardrobe to a minimum and carry correspondingly smaller bags. If small enough, these bags could be carried aboard by passengers and stored either under or adjacent to their seats. Many planes provide for this now.

One night I boarded a plane at New York's International Airport, with a conference scheduled the next morning in Los Angeles. As the plane taxied to the runway and waited its turn to take off, I mentioned that I was tired and the stewardess suggested I retire. I undressed, took a mild sedative, went to my berth, and immediately fell asleep. I don't know what awakened me, perhaps it was the absolute stillness. For a moment I had the feeling I was dead and in another world. I rang for the stewardess, but no one came. I rang again, longer. Again there was no response, so I got out of the berth and padded up the aisle. The cabin was empty, so was the cockpit. I got to the door and located a ground attendant, who was just as surprised as I was. Owing to weather conditions, the flight had been canceled. Hidden behind the curtains of my berth, I was the forgotten man.

CHAPTER 9.

THEY said it would never replace the horse, but more and more it looks as if the automobile is here to stay.

At last count, 43,811,260 of these frowning, space-eating, two-eyed beetles were prowling the 3,300,000 miles of the nation's highways and streets, running up an aggregate of 521,000,000,000 miles annually. In southern California, where there is the highest concentration of automobile traffic anywhere in the world, one in every three residents has a car and most of the rest can hardly wait until they can afford the down payment.

Food, shelter, and clothing used to be the three basic necessities, but now a fourth, the automobile, has been added. Indeed, many normal adult males put their cars first. The flashy monster that lives in the garage, likely as not, is man's most cherished possession, almost in a category with the electric train of his boyhood. It is even a serious threat to the dog as man's best friend. And a car is not merely transportation; it is a gleaming symbol of its owner's station in life and a reflection of his personality. He will expound proudly to his friends on its speed, power, getaway, and low

THE OPEN ROAD

appearance. The first dent in the fender is a tragedy of the first magnitude. The carburetor mixture is more intensely explored than his first-born's formula.

When a man buys or builds a home, he usually thinks in terms of living there a long time. He gives careful study to the number of bedrooms, he wants a certain-sized living room, he may insist on a barbecue pit. His decision is made slowly and conservatively. This caution disappears when he buys an automobile. As if blinded by the glittering chrome, he may select, on sudden impulse, a racy extreme model. Above all else, it is on wheels, and if his taste or the trend changes, he knows he can dispose of it at the nearest car lot.

Surveys show that he wants the ultimate luxury of the moment in his automobile, regardless of cost. Manufacturers offer a line of models of each brand, and increasingly the de luxe cars outsell the austere. Sixty per cent of the sales of one brand are in the top bracket, $3376, only forty per cent in the stripped-down $2323 job. In several other lines, the ratio is eighty-five to fifteen in favor of the more expensive cars.

As a car owner, I am impressed with the excellence of my automobile's mechanism, its safety, its brakes, the weight and balance that keep all four wheels on the ground on a sharp turn. I am grateful for the moments of privacy it gives me in a life crowded with deadlines, conferences, and telephone calls. I appreciate its durability and its reliability. It is a dutiful servant, quietly responsive to my touch.

As an industrial designer, I find that my car leaves a great deal to be desired. It is sleek and powerful-looking, but it is not beautiful in the sense that form should follow function. And, quite obviously, Joe and Josephine, as we know them, weren't around when the shell was devised. In many cars, if the driver isn't careful he'll bump his head as he enters. He may have to squirm to get into the seat behind the wheel. He may crack his ankle as he gets out. He may find his visibility obstructed.

The reason for these outright errors in design may be found in the nature of the gigantic and fabulous automotive industry itself. The automobile grew like Topsy and looks like Turvy. The Chrysler Airflow was a failure in 1936 because the public wasn't ready to accept it. A few years later, automobile body designers were emphasizing a similar exterior air-streaming at the expense of everything else, although it is pretty generally known that air-streaming is needless in the average family car. But having set the lines, they had no alternative but to squeeze the passenger into the interior as best they could without sacrificing the low sleekness the public considers essential.

Behind this acceptance, of course, were mammoth exploitation campaigns. Repeated double-spread magazine

128

ads, radio commercials, TV extravaganzas, newspaper sections, and traveling shows can have tremendous impact, and it is understandable that, under this onslaught, people have become eager to own these magnificent Gargantuas, to the point of skimping on food, shelter, and clothing and taking on long-term installment payments.

Truly, the manufacturers could sell anything. When the 1948 Cadillac appeared with its rear fishtails, some people laughed. The fishtails seemed out of place, almost an offense to the eye. In a few years of steamroller exploitation, however, they have become a symbol of quality, widely copied by the competition.

A<small>N</small> innovation in automobile design doesn't stay new long, for Detroit plays a follow-the-leader game. Successful new features are carefully guarded, but somehow the secrets get out and similar novelties frequently appear on competitive cars at the same time. A manufacturer has only a year's protection, according to agreement, before a rival can copy such things as power steering, a bent all-vision windshield, or an electrically controlled seat.

I am aware that these statements appear to be those of a frustrated industrial designer sitting in a corner eating a bunch of sour grapes and spitting the seeds at Detroit. Such is not the case, for I was retained three years in an automobile manufacturing plant. It must be added that I accomplished absolutely nothing, and it was not that I didn't try or that my client was lacking in patience. The reason was simply that the business was so vast and successful that it was con-sidered unwise to interrupt the tradition of smoothness and gleam when all that had to be done was to add more of what it already had. And in spite of my rude complaints, and considering the hodgepodge manner in which they must work, automobile designers have achieved a minor miracle of integration.

Auto-body designers, of course, are faced with a paradox. They are expected to create a vehicle that will conform to an established concept—that of giving precedence to the exterior form—yet that will also insure comfort and adequate visibility for the passengers. This seems to me to be approaching the problem backward. The first step should be to seat five persons scientifically and comfortably on the chassis and build the car around them, after a thorough study of their anatomies in the various positions they would occupy in the car. The resulting design would preclude the present discomforts.

My dream car of the future need not go 150 miles an hour or drip with chrome or have leopard upholstery. Instead, serious thought should go into safety and creature comforts. For instance, some foolproof system of taking the glare out of night driving will be devised. In the interest of improved rear visibility, a wide-angled periscope might be installed, opening up the entire expanse in back of the car. Good posture is impossible in some cars at present because of the insistence on lowness. Not long ago I rode in a 1908 Rolls-Royce and, although it was relatively antiquated in other ways, I could sit erect in a relaxed position, without knocking off my hat, and see out on all four sides. Someday perhaps a simple method of parking can be devised, so that a motorist can drive alongside a vacant space, lower a set of retractable wheels set at a right angle, and glide to the curb.

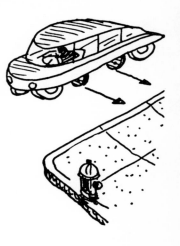

Occasionally I visit the fabulous factories that mass-produce automobiles. I find the ingenuity and efficiency a breath-taking sight. To see shiny, smooth, upholstered cars emerge from the seeming turmoil of a production line is a thing of wonder, almost like the miracle of birth itself. Yet my inclination is to shout above the noise, "Hold that line!" and to point out to someone that there are glaring mistakes in the cars pouring out of the factory. What Detroit pur-veys in car design enormously influences trends in taste, far beyond the horizon of the automobile. An absurd design element having nothing to do with efficiency or beauty of the car, promoted into acceptance, may be imitated shame-lessly on toasters and typewriters. There again it may be successful, but it is still bad design.

In spite of what I have said here, the automotive design world is not all wilderness. Raymond Loewy's first post-war Studebaker was a car that reflected its honesty, and, as I see it, has led the whole industry several steps along the path toward intelligent design.

WHATEVER their appearance, automobiles have crowded into all our lives, creating problems far beyond the length of the wheelbase in a dealer's showroom. They have become a mixed blessing. A person can drive on good highways from coast to coast, from border to border, and see the cities, the mountains, the deserts, the rivers— the glories of America known previously only on picture postcards. Autos are a godsend for persons living in isolated places and an irreplaceable convenience for those in widespread metropolitan areas. But they have also become a menace. With each new car on the highway, a new hazard is created. There is no longer any such thing as absolute safety, only comparative safety.

In 1953, 38,300 persons were killed and 1,350,000 injured in auto accidents in the United States. In the three-year Korean war, there were 25,604 battle deaths and 103,492 nonmortal wounds. The Korean war is over, but the highway slaughter continues year after year.

The blame for this carnage must be placed partially on cars that are too fast and powerful in the hands of reckless or inconsiderate drivers, but also on inadequately planned highways and the nerve-racking congestion of our city streets. The great freeways and turnpikes that crisscross the country and slice the cities are triumphs of engineering and a great boon in unscrambling traffic congestion, but they can also be as deadly as gunfire. They are responsible for a condition known as highway hypnosis. A motorist with his eyes fixed on the unchanging road ahead, listening to the monotonous drone of his engine, can go into a kind of trance. Unless his attention is diverted, he may lose his sense of proportion and collide head-on with an oncoming car when he unwisely tries to pass a slower-moving car. Or he may smash into the slower car ahead, and in an instant a dozen speeding cars may telescope into each other. If it were not so full of horror, such an accident would have a comic-book humor.

Someday cars may be equipped with a radar device that will warn drivers of the proximity of the car in front and even automatically decelerate their engines. Until then, other devices must be found to forestall highway hypnosis. Advertising billboards have been criticized off many roads, but they do break the monotony in a horrible sort of way. Large beds of colorful flowers or flowering shrubs or groves of trees, which could be illuminated at night, are a good equivalent. An occasional piece of sculpture or a quarter-mile-long picture wall graphically highlighting the history or major occupation or scenic beauty of the area would also afford relief. Various colors might be integrated into the surfacing of the highway, or the texture of the road might be varied to give a change in sound as the tires rolled over it. Highway hypnosis is a field still to be explored and counteracted. So is that other psychosomatic phenomenon, traffic nerves, which afflicts those who navigate their cars through the snailike traffic of the city streets. Expanded off-street parking and more scientific traffic handling are part of the answer—but these haven't managed to keep pace with the steadily increasing number of Americans on wheels. Smaller cars and taxis will someday tend to relieve the pressure, but their universal use is far away.

THE newer freeways have provision for off-highway parking in case of emergencies and telephones at frequent intervals, but the basic oasis for motorists in both country and city will doubtless continue to be the service station. A quarter million of such havens dot the country, and they have become a refreshing phase of motoring.

Long ago, the wise men of the petroleum industry realized that one gasoline looks the same as another. The consumer rarely sees it at all. To compete intelligently, there-

133

fore, it was advisable to give the product a personality through good service and facilities. Today they know they are selling service, and it is not accidental that smiling, friendly, efficient men check oil, water, and air, change tires, clean windows, sell accessories, furnish maps and directions, even suggest good hotels and eating places, if requested. The service station has become a beacon on our highways, and the polite, uniformed attendant is an American institution. Pumping gas almost seems the least of his duties.

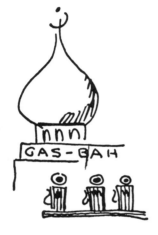

The building itself must be the acme of neatness, providing spotless rest rooms, beverages, cigarettes, and in some instances everything from food to nylon stockings. Like most architecture, the service station has gone through cycles. Thirty years ago it was a depressing shanty. The sudden mushrooming of the industry gave rise to all kinds of outlandish structures—Moorish castles, pagodas, log cabins, grounded airplanes. The next trend was toward a stark rectangular box, its sterility relieved by colored stripes and signs, several miles of neon tubing, and enough paper-streamer advertising to conceal the lack of architecture Worse, many major companies followed the identical pattern, so that recognizing a particular company's station made it necessary to read a sign or memorize a color scheme.

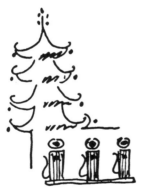

Sanity has taken hold in the last few years, and we have seen a race for identity and attention. Oil-company executives know that shape and color and design are vital factors in making motorists stop at their station. As a result, today's backdrop for roadside service is a carefully planned piece of

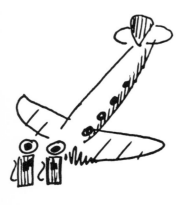

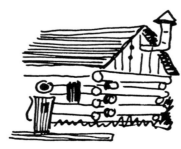

architecture, not only efficient but eye-arresting and in good taste. Reproduced in great numbers, well-designed service stations subtly influence the nation's architecture.

Our client in this field is Cities Service. Working with their marketing, architectural, and engineering groups, we have developed typical stations that have a family resemblance easily recognizable to motorists. It was our job to integrate a great many intangibles and tangibles. After all, much of what the company has to sell doesn't come in a package. To accomplish this integration, two men from our office put on uniforms and worked at a service station to get firsthand knowledge of customer reactions and to find out the hard and dirty way what convenience could be added to perfect the service. Not merely the architecture was studied, but all the station's facilities—the tank trucks that deliver the fuel, the cans containing the oil, the signs, the availability of the air and water hoses. To indoctrinate ourselves before starting the design program, we visited the company's oil wells, the pipe lines, the tanker transportation, the cracking plants, the storage tanks, and the laboratories. We found that everyone from the executive in his paneled office to the grimy foreman at the wellhead was dedicated to the goal of producing a superior product.

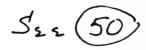

The fuel, servicing, and maintenance phase of driving has been pretty well resolved, but automobile design and the traffic maelstroms that afflict the big cities have not. Nevertheless, there's hope that, with sanity and planning and patience, order will someday be brought out of the chaos.

CHAPTER 10. DESIGN

WE HAVE worked on freight cars, a lollypop packing machine, an auto tire, a linotype machine, magazine typography and make-up, an egg-candling machine, the interior of the Perisphere at the New York World's Fair, a fly swatter, a sonar fish finder, a button stitching machine for men's coats, a women's urinal, a Geiger counter, a cigarette-making machine, Diesel engines, a vault door, and a thermostat for barns to insure the contentment of cows and chickens.

These may seem far afield from the ordinary pastures of the industrial designer; actually, they are further evidence that industrial design is an expanding profession and that a good design, whether in a piece of machinery or on a printed page, expresses the integrity of the product and is, perhaps intangibly, a trade-mark of quality. If a tractor appears well put together outwardly, it is logical to assume that the internal mechanism is equally sturdy. A dealer, after looking at a new tractor design, once told me, "If it works as well as it looks, I'll buy it."

Naturally, some persons will ask what difference it makes whether a John Deere combine is well designed. Why get fancy about a behemoth that is used for a rough task? To say

IN UNEXPECTED PLACES

this is to admit a lack of awareness of what has been taking place—in this case, down on the farm.

There are few farmers or farmers' wives as we used to know them. More often than not, the modern farmer has been to agricultural school. He doesn't plant by the moon any more. He is an engineer of sorts and knows all about tractors, corn pickers, cotton pickers, combines, choppers, blowers, balers, land shapers, and manure spreaders—and these days may even pilot his own plane or helicopter for crop dusting or fast business and pleasure trips. He has acquired the implements most suited to his needs and he knows how to operate and maintain them. If he has a large farm, there will likely be a well-equipped machine shop on it to keep those implements in working order. It would be disastrous for a piece of equipment to conk out at harvest time. A good farmer is more interested in the engine of his tractor than he is in the purr of his Cadillac.

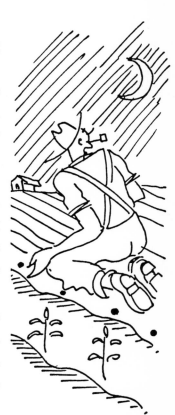

The farmer's wife also has many devices to make her work easier. She no longer spends laborious hours in canning—she deep-freezes food for the entire year. She has all the hot water she needs, and she doesn't have to depend on the whim of an old-style windmill to get it and then heat it on the stove.

She has the same automatic washers and cleaners found in the homes of her city cousins, and probably a car of her own, too. The milkmaid or hired hand has been replaced by mechanical milkers.

Farm machinery has come a long way since the primitive days of the all-purpose tractor pulling a variety of ungainly attachments. More and more of these attachments are integrated with the tractor and can be raised and lowered and controlled by a hydraulic system. Today the sale of a tractor depends heavily on how well integrated it is with the equipment that does the actual farming operation. The trend is away from cumbersome, hand-built equipment bearing the unmistakable thumbprint of the blacksmith and toward precision-built machinery, the appearance of which bespeaks the modern factory from which it came.

O NE of the first indications that the public's taste had become discriminating in buying heavy machinery was in the farm-implement business, and it has spread in all directions in the last few years. Some of our most important clients today build turret lathes, bushings for high-voltage power lines, packaging machinery, lift trucks, oil-well drilling machinery, and torque converters.

Working in a field we never dreamed of invading, we were able to demonstrate to manufacturers of heavy machinery that a well-planned product, no matter what it was, would sell better than a poorly planned one. They got not merely a better-looking lathe or packaging machine, but one that inspired pride of ownership in its operators, who, therefore, kept it in top condition.

138

pictures on pages 48 + 49

We worked on a deep-well turbine pump for Byron Jackson. With their engineers we were able to relocate the small but vital oil reservoir from the outside of the motor housing to the inside of the base casting, so that it lubricated the bearing more efficiently. This improvement gave the pump the look that has come to be associated with modern integrated machinery. Incidentally, the oil-reservoir cover was adapted to serve a dual purpose and became the name plate, at a saving of cost.

Another instance of design off the beaten path was our work on a spectacular display for the National Supply Company, manufacturers of equipment for the petroleum industry, with whose engineers we have collaborated on the appearance of many products. Many months before the mammoth Tulsa Oil Show, National Supply's management summoned me to discuss their exhibit.

After a daylong session with thirty National Supply executives, a design was evolved centering around the familiar oilwell derrick, surrounded with a doughnut-shaped glass building, which appeared to float ten feet off the ground. The inside of the room, comfortably furnished, would provide relief for weary feet. National Supply products would be displayed on the ground level, and the hook and drills that operated the turntable would be suspended from the derrick. Access to this unorthodox room would be by a picturesque ramp. In short, we would reverse the usual procedure. The customer would be in the air-conditioned showcase, looking out at the merchandise.

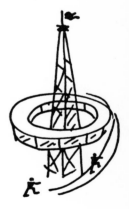

The Goodyear Tire Company came to us many years ago and asked if we could improve the appearance of their tires.

They wanted them distinctive but kept in harmony with the designs of all cars.

After several months, we presented a full-size plaster model of our design to the directors of the company, and they accepted it. At lunch that day a Goodyear executive remarked with engaging frankness that he liked our design but thought we had been overpaid. After all, he said, it was a simple design, just a lot of concentric loops around the wall of the tire. He happened to be coming to New York the following week, and I invited him to visit our office. When he came in, I showed him more than sixty sketches and fourteen full-size plaster models of tires—some fancy, some simple, some extreme. When I explained why we had done all that work before determining the final design, he understood the basis for our fee.

Soon after I opened my industrial-design office, Otis L. Wiese, editor and publisher of *McCall's Magazine*, sent for me. He had seen the settings we had done for Jerome Kern's musical, *The Cat and the Fiddle*, and thought that the kind of approach that had gone into them could be applied to the magazine.

Magazines in those days, particularly the homemaking magazines, had little visual appeal. By far the best-looking part of them was the advertising. A dull sameness characterized the layout of the editorial pages. One reason was that the artists, after reading the stories, selected the scenes they thought best to illustrate. It was usually the climactic kiss between Him and Her. As a result, the magazines had little over-all impact or pace.

140

When I first walked into Wiese's office I was as astonished at his youth as he was at mine. We were both in our mid-twenties. I told him that I knew nothing about typography, engraving, or printing, but that I was interested in tackling the job. If his people would finance my education in these fields for a year, I said, I would submit a dummy containing my ideas. To my surprise, they agreed to pay me to study the magazine business.

I went to Elmer Adler, a man I had long admired but had never met. Adler was chief typographical consultant for *The New York Times* for many years and published the *Colophon,* the monthly journal of the fine printing business. He was enchanted with my belief that I could learn all about the printing industry in a year and agreed to spend three nights a week with me, guiding my education. He also made available to me his fine library of old books and type specimens.

I traveled to Dayton, Ohio, where *McCall's* was printed, to learn about their presses, so that I wouldn't suggest any innovations that were mechanically impossible. I spent many days at *McCall's* Stamford, Connecticut, plant, watching plates being engraved. I fought my way through several years of back issues of *McCall's, Ladies' Home Journal, Woman's Home Companion, Good Housekeeping, Vogue,* and *Harper's Bazaar.*

When I decided upon the approach I wanted to make, I took the schedule for an issue under preparation and read all the manuscripts going into it—not only the stories, but the articles about cooking, decoration, fashions, and babies —and converted them into a new kind of format.

Six months after our first meeting, I presented Wiese with a dummy of the entire magazine. He was enthusiastic about it, and it was adopted as *McCall's* new format. The owners of the magazine invited me to stay on indefinitely, but I declined, asking only to remain the rest of the year to see if my formula was workable. However, I became fascinated with the challenge of creating a new product each month and of meeting the awakened competition and stayed twelve years, reading every story and article, and sitting in on editorial conferences three times a week.

It was physically possible for me to carry out this demanding assignment—along with my work in the theater and other industrial-design jobs—only because *McCall's* provided a top-flight assistant and a complete staff, who took much of the load off my back.

The *McCall's* formula that emerged was based on the concept of the entire magazine, not merely the first fifteen or twenty pages, as the "canvas" for more striking art and type displays. It released the art director from traditions in type, artwork, and color and enabled him to achieve a pattern and pace by alternating pages of quiet and rest with pages containing big punches. At first there were complaints that the new layout frames restricted the freedom of artists, but the best illustrators agreed with us and we consulted with them before we confined their work to a certain shape or size. Part of the formula also was that two facing pages should be considered an entity and designed as such, an accepted practice in layout work today.

We worked briefly for several other magazines. Henry Luce wanted a critical analysis of *Life* and *Time*, and after sitting in the publication office as an observer for several months, I recommended, in essence, more pace and pattern but few changes in typography. Luce was anxious to have people read both *Life* and *Time* from cover to cover, an important factor in selling advertising. Many of our thoughts had to do with this. We also prevailed upon *Time* to take the "spinach" off the cover, to simplify the type, and to identify the cover portraits more specifically. Many of them were of people whose names and work were known, but whose faces weren't. A background sketch, sometimes an abstraction, identifying the person with his work, served the purpose.

We were also called in by DeWitt Wallace, editor of the fabulously successful *Reader's Digest*. Some of the layout suggestions resulting from our study were accepted by Wallace and his staff and still are discernible in the *Digest*.

An amiable stranger came into our New York office one day, and we chatted about politics, the weather, and the problems arising from living in New York. He didn't come to any particular point and, as I was busy, I said finally, "Is there something I can do for you?" He replied, "I've heard of you and I just wondered if you could design a fly swatter for me." As we talked, I doodled a design. He thought it was fine and offered payment. I declined, explaining that no effort had been involved. He said he was head of the United States Manufacturing Company of Decatur, Illinois, which made 20,000,000 fly swatters a year. I was amazed at the figure, and he explained that for some unknown reason people don't save fly swatters, but buy new ones each summer. He was certain the new design would increase that figure and departed, saying that I would hear from him. I thought nothing further of the incident until, months later, sizable royalty checks began to arrive.

As everyone knows, the Trylon and Perisphere, designed by Wallace Harrison, became the symbol of the 1939 New York World's Fair. The directors of the Fair invited me to work out the interior of the two-hundred-foot-diameter globe, the largest sphere ever constructed. It had been suggested that this huge interior be separated into forty-eight areas, one for each state, and these were to be adorned with plaques, musty firearms, tattered flags, and other authentic, commemorative historical articles. I balked at the idea of inflicting such a boring display on the public and suggested instead that the theme of the Fair, the Interdependence of Man, be dramatized inside the entire sphere without destroying the awesome effect of the mammoth ball by subdividing it. This concept was executed. Thousands of spectators were carried to the equator line of the globe on two of the longest escalators ever assembled. There they entered the spherical structure on one of two ringlike platforms that seemed suspended in space one above the other. The platforms made a revolution every eight minutes, by which time the spectators were gently eased off. The crowds, thus completely controlled, looked down on a utopian city with its planned work area and residence sections. The cycle of day and night was reproduced and, to an especially composed musical score, mammoth moving pictures of singing and marching workers of the world converged in the center, collaborating to make a better world of tomorrow.

While in a California swimming pool one December day, I was called to the telephone. It was one of the executives of the Hilton Hotels, calling from New York, asking if we would do over the *décor* of the Persian Room, occupying a ground-floor corner of the Plaza Hotel. Having frequently been a patron in the famous room, I was pleased at the opportunity.

More than appearance is involved in remodeling and redecorating a night club. The industrial designer must think also in terms of air conditioning, lighting, easy access for the waiters through crowded tables, acoustics, fire exits—but always glamour. The most popular night spots are those in which the lighting magically erases wrinkles and double chins, making dowagers look like debutantes and tired merchants feel like Olympic champions.

Our examination of the room recalled the excavations of the site of ancient Troy. Four successive designers over a period of forty years had imposed their ideas on the room, but, unfortunately, the last three had not bothered to remove the previous interiors, which nested one inside the other. In order to enlarge the capacity and satisfy a critical municipal building code and fire department, the four interiors were removed, and we got a fresh start from the brick walls. We settled on a diagonal plan that would give every seat a good view. The bandstand, therefore, was placed in one corner, and everything fanned out from it.

Our design was contemporary, but with a Persian motif chosen because of the famous name of the room, and for this we visited museums and haunted the Iranian Institute, reading the lore of Iran and studying Persian temples and miniatures. The Persian room has eight enormous windows twenty feet high on two of its walls. For these we had curtains woven of deep blue and green with metallic strands. I requested Dorothy Liebes, who was doing the fabric, to interweave thousands of tiny electric-light bulbs of the type used in delicate surgical instruments. These flickering lights simulated the flight of fireflies during certain dance numbers. It was a long time before the weavers got over being bemused at this unprecedented alliance of the electrician's trade and their craft.

THERE has been little new development in bank-vault doors in the last fifty years. Our directive from the Mosler Safe Company was to incorporate their engineering staff's improvements into a new concept that would reflect modern banking and contemporary architecture, yet still give the customer the feeling of security that is essential to the renters of safe-deposit boxes. The completed vault door is functional and presents the very epitome of protection. During the course of our work on the main vault door, I made the casual observation that the grilled gate that swings just behind the vault door was incongruous with the new design. Its seven uptilted pikes, ready to impale anyone who tried to climb over it, looked as if they were straight from ancient Rome. In considering possible modification of the piked gate, it was determined that four and one half inches was the maximum opening at the top and bottom that would exclude intruders. The final design filled the opening, and the pikes were discarded. Curiously enough, close examination of the original piked gate revealed that a pint-sized Joe or Josephine might conceivably have squeezed through the seven-inch clearance at the bottom.

picture on page (51)

Along with almost everything else down on the farm, the old barn isn't what it used to be. The litter of hay and oats, the old, broken tools and cultivator, the battered harness, are gone. Everything is neat and in place. The Minneapolis-Honeywell Regulator Company, alert to the trend toward scientific orderliness, even had us work on a bright-red thermostat, known as the Farm-O-Stat, to control the ventilating fans in barns, poultry houses, milkhouses, and banana rooms. It is large, rugged, and dust- and corrosion-resistant, providing living-room comfort for old Dobbin.

At any given moment around the clock, many thousands of people are aloft in airplanes, traveling for business, pleasure, or on an emergency. Their safety depends to a great degree on the vigilance of the men in the Civil Aeronautics Administration control towers around the country. These men are charged with the responsibility of knowing where every plane is every moment it's in the air, guiding it through storms and fog and away from danger. They maintain communications with each other and with all planes in flight by phone, radio, and teletype.

Because of the great increase in air traffic since World War II, the CAA retained the Bell Telephone Laboratories to make a comprehensive study of air-traffic control with a view toward greater efficiency. Our office was called in to analyze the relationship of the men in the control towers and the equipment they use and the psychological influences that prevail. We undertook a personal survey of eleven control centers throughout the nation, to learn about existing equipment and the reactions of personnel. Armed with this basic knowledge we co-operated with Bell Laboratories engi-

147

neers in studying personnel comfort, acoustics, color, visibility, illumination, circulation and volume of traffic. Our thoughts were developed on paper, then accurate small-scale models were prepared to illustrate our proposals and to crystallize further thinking. Plans for an improved network of CAA towers are ready for the age of jet aircraft.

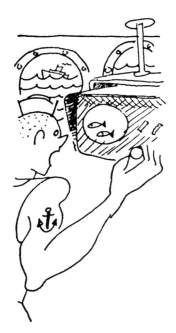

ANOTHER unusual design assignment in an unexpected place was the sea scanner for Minneapolis-Honeywell. Mounted in the cabin of a boat, the device gives a visual record of any solid bodies within a diameter of 2400 feet. Sound impulses are reflected back on striking a solid object and can be observed on a radar screen. The scanner can be used in navigation, underwater surveying, mapping, and to find fish. We suggested the use of a rugged cast-aluminum case for the recording instrument instead of sheet metal, arranging the control panels in a logical and functional order, and setting the scope so that a light shield was built in rather than affixed to the outside. Tuna boats operating out of West Coast ports have found the sea scanner extremely accurate and valuable in detecting the elusive chicken of the sea.

A lift truck is a small, stubby vehicle capable of hoisting four thousand pounds and is used in warehouse and supply areas. It must be compact but powerful, have a minimum turning radius, and be extremely maneuverable in reverse as well as forward. An industrial designer's talents ordinarily might not be considered essential in such a vehicle, but we were called in by the Hyster Company to work on its famous line. The temptation was to give the

Hyster trucks a racy appearance, but, after study, we decided on a look of simple, rugged functionalism, with improved safety, visibility, and maintenance factors. After all, they are husky warehouse lift trucks needed to do a workhorse job for a long time, not nervous fillies out to break a track record.

Many years ago I was sent to Sioux City, Iowa, by RKO. The luxurious, new RKO theater there was not doing very good business, but the older, plainer rival theater down the street, showing inferior pictures, was jammed. No one could understand why. I mingled with the theatergoers and listened to their comments, and the reason became clear. It seemed that the farmers and workmen were self-conscious about coming into the de luxe lobby with their wet, muddy shoes, for fear of soiling the deep, rich carpeting. We took up the carpets, replaced them with rubber mats, and business increased overnight.

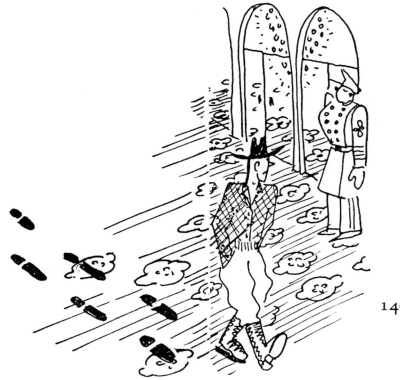

149

CHAPTER 11. WORKING

ON military projects, the industrial designer's procedure remains the same as on commercial assignments, but there is a shift in emphasis. Instead of profits for the client, the goal in government work is a contribution to morale, the intangible force that impels soldiers to have confidence and pride in their weapons and therefore in themselves and that, in the long pull, wins battles and wars.

The industrial designer strengthens this force by giving military weapons added safety, utility, ease of maintenance, and convenience and comfort. Our particular role was pointedly expressed by a phrase in our contract with the Navy to redesign the interiors of certain ships. A naval legal aide wrote that we were to "improve the habitability" aboard these ships. To a great extent, the phrase applies also to the service we rendered other military projects—transportation vehicles, specialized anti-aircraft protective devices, combat vehicles, tank interiors, the control devices and consoles on the guided missile known as Nike, and a sturdy naval icebreaker.

FOR THE GOVERNMENT

OUR concern is a more efficient integration of man and equipment, and we are dealing again with Joe and Josephine. There are Joe's reflexes to consider, his reactions to heat and cold and light and dark, and his anatomical proportions. Josephine, who in this instance wears the uniform of a WAC, a WAVE, or a lady Marine, comes in for attention, too. And while the profit motive is deleted from our design efforts, cost is not. Even when morale is at stake, we weigh every penny. But we know that good form and proportion and color need not cost anything extra, and if we spend money improving a gun or a bunk, we can usually balance the expenditure in reduced cost of maintenance. And certainly money is well spent when it eliminates the things a man might trip over or catch his fingers and legs in and so become seriously maimed.

In some instances, we have worked directly with the military, in others we have been called in by our regular clients who hold defense contracts. Occasionally a manufacturer who had never thought of using our services on his peacetime products would summon us on a war job. We did extensive work in radar equipment for bombers and fighters and for trailer-mounted field equipment for anti-aircraft detection. Shortly after the outbreak of World War II, our office was assigned to make a compact arrangement of the many complicated components of the cumbersome 105-mm. anti-aircraft gun. By reorganizing these components, the crucial period between the change-over from traveling position to firing position was reduced from fifteen to three-and-one-half minutes. Minutes can save lives in battle.

SEE page 51

O NE of the most interesting problems assigned our office during the last war was designing a suite of strategy rooms for the Joint Chiefs of Staff, Generals Marshall and Arnold and Admirals King and Leahy. In this holy of holies, the top brass would be quickly briefed on critical engagements as the action took place, and would also study the global aspects of the war through visual presentations. The setup was resolved into two large rooms identical in size and parallel in the long dimension, and a small workshop for preparation of material and storage of maps. Also adjacent was a "file" of sliding four-by-eight-foot screens arranged so that they could be pulled out on tracks. One screen could be used, or a series of screens buckled together, with transparent overlays showing essential data pinned to them.

A world map, accurate and up to date, was painted on a curved, metal-clad surface, twenty-five feet long and twelve feet high, on a wall of one of the main rooms. To prevent the wear and tear that comes from concentrated pin-pushing, tiny colored magnets were substituted for conventional pins. A projector was also trained on the map so that slides, when inserted, graphically depicted actions anywhere in the world or indicated weather conditions or other desired information. The other room was for projection of 16-mm. motion pictures, still pictures, and drawings.

The request for these strategy rooms came from Washington and carried the proviso that they be in operation in six weeks. This would have been a Herculean task in peacetime; in wartime Washington it seemed impossible.

The original proposal was to erect a building, but this idea was abandoned because of lack of materials and the time limit. After exploring existing government buildings, we located an auditorium in the U. S. Public Health Building on Constitution Avenue that was large enough to contain these rooms. We removed the chandeliers and draperies and arranged for materials through a top White House priority. New York seemed the obvious place to "invent" these rooms, and a quick search turned up a mammoth scenic studio that had been converted from an old brewery. The area was comparable to the space in the Washington auditorium, and within the next few hectic weeks the rooms came to life. The floor, walls, and ceilings were built in sections so that they could be easily taken apart and reassembled.

Floors, walls and ceilings—even mobile ones with the flexibility of an Erector set—constituted the relatively simple part of the problem, however. The real jigsaw puzzle lay in planning, procurement and installation of security devices, soundproofing, air conditioning, a telephone system, several means of still and motion-picture projection, and a

153

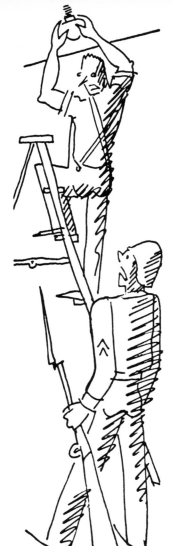

complicated lighting system. All this had to be put together and placed in working order in New York and reassembled on the shores of the Potomac. During each step of the building, knocking down, and rebuilding, innumerable Marine guards stood by to make certain no listening device or explosive was slipped into the woodwork. Before the rooms were sent to Washington, a group of military men were invited to come up to our old brewery to inspect them and to try out the various devices that had been provided. I am sure that none of these gentlemen, who conducted their tour in a most leisurely fashion, realized that our time schedule was so tight that we had trucks waiting outside the building ready to haul the rooms to Washington the instant they could be taken apart and loaded.

It's no secret that the task force in our office that handled the pressure assignment used whatever means it found available for this command performance. The genius and experience of Hollywood and Rochester were called in to help devise the best visual presentation, and the A-1 priority enabled us to "borrow" some otherwise unprocurable equipment from a battleship. Even the bowling alley was a source for us. This was in connection with the solution of a problem in impromptu cartography. How could it be made possible for one man to draw a map, or delineate his thoughts on a map, and still have twenty or thirty observers see clearly what he was doing? In such a situation, inevitably everyone is in the line of vision of everyone else. The answer came one day when I remembered seeing a device used by bowlers to project their scores on a screen. We procured several of these machines and by means of relatively simple revisions made it possible for the strategists to project their map work on a screen as they developed it on a desk in front of them.

The important thing was that the strategy rooms were completed and furnished, down to the ash trays, within a month, and the Big Four of U. S. strategy had an adequate place to see the war as it was and make future plans.

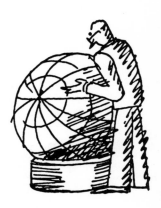

ALSO during the war, a request came from Washington for four globes of the world more than thirteen feet in circumference and revolvable in any direction. Aluminum being unavailable, the globes were constructed of laminated hoops of cherrywood, doweled every six inches to prevent expansion and contraction, and covered with detailed maps of the world drawn by the National Geographic Society. To permit the globes to turn easily, we at first considered a pool of mercury in which they would float, but this was discarded because mercury is poisonous. Experiment proved that a "cup" of hard rubber balls working against steel balls gave the same easy action. Only on the day of delivery did our "clients" become known to us—President Roosevelt and Prime Minister Churchill, Marshal Stalin, and the U. S. Army.

Years later, when we were doing the *Independence* and the *Constitution*, these globes were reproduced with the U. S. Army's permission and today occupy prominent positions in the libraries aboard these vessels. The motion of a ship at sea demanded a more secure fastening than our rubber-ball bearings, and the globes are held in the traditional gimbals. Somehow it is more gratifying to see passengers pointing out their home towns in Iowa or Idaho than imagining the Big Three studying the Battle of the Bulge.

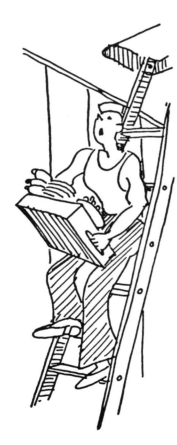

ANOTHER challenging project came as a result of a contract with the Navy to "improve the habitability" aboard the 2200-ton DD 692 class World War II destroyers. As originally designed, these ships had adequate room for officers and men, but as the technology of warfare added new space-consuming equipment, more men were required to operate and maintain them. In 1950, the Navy began an intensive program to correct the resultant crowding on shipboard.

One of the first steps, after studying a survey made by the Operational Development Force, was to send two members of our staff on a voyage on one of the "tin cans." Their time and motion studies were discouraging.

We discovered that an average of only thirty-one of the eighty-eight seats in the mess hall were in use at one time. This was owing partly to the inaccessibility of some seats, but largely to the fact that the men averaged only ten and one-half minutes in eating a meal—some bolting their food in as little as two minutes flat. (By comparison, a large cafeteria chain has determined that the average time required by its customers for a meal is twenty minutes.) This unseemly haste was inspired not only by the food served, but also by the discomfort, heat and noise in the room. We also found that time was wasted in the mess line because food had to be carried in large traylike receptacles from one deck to another—a difficult feat in a rough sea.

We found the quarters badly overcrowded. The space

between berths both vertically and horizontally was so tight that a man could barely turn around or over, and an average of five minutes was required to empty a berthing compartment on the sounding of general quarters. Destroyers have sunk in less time.

The sanitary facilities were antiquated and lacking in privacy. The arrangement of lockers necessitated arousing the occupants of lower berths when access was wanted. There was virtually no recreation space for officers or men. Storage space for clothing was inadequate. Pipe, wiring, and vent ducts ran through the compartments in a disorderly manner. Lighting was poor, ventilation bad and temperatures were high.

In a cramped space of a 2200-ton destroyer, there is a limit to what can be done. No wings or annexes can be added to the exterior. When a bulkhead is moved to enlarge one space, it means the adjacent area is that much smaller. The problem of improved habitability becomes one of robbing Peter to pay Paul. We made half-inch scale models of the various compartments, and moved blocks of wood representing necessary furniture and equipment in a three-dimensional jigsaw puzzle until a more efficient arrangement was achieved.

In the crew berthing area, the furniture and equipment were rearranged to improve ease of movement and give more space for dressing. Individual privacy was increased by using the lockers as dividers and providing canvas shields to be hung between berths. Writing tables were installed where possible. Piping and ducts were rerouted so they were reduced as obstructions to circulation and vision. Ventilated collection bins were provided for soiled clothing, which previously had been gathered in large canvas bags that obstructed passageways. Particularly appreciated by the ship's crew was the installation of individual berth reading lights.

As usual, color was an important ally in the renovation. The Navy places a limit on the variety of colors because of logistics, and we kept our palette to five shades. By using them scientifically as well as decoratively, close quarters were made to appear to expand, and piping and ducts became less apparent. Rooms were made more relaxing, and a cheerful atmosphere was added.

Since compartments on a destroyer receive little daylight, artificial illumination is necessary. Mostly bare, glaring incandescent bulbs were in use, although they give insufficient light and are fatiguing to the eyes. Our recommendation for installing fluorescent fixtures was accepted.

THE habitability study was made on the *Gyatt*, and shortly after it was submitted to the Bureau of Ships, we were given another contract to apply it to the *Meredith*, a sister ship then in drydock at the Norfolk Naval Shipyard, Portsmouth, Virginia.

As work progressed, problems appeared. Solutions that had looked fine on paper struck snags—immovable pipes, ladders, escape hatches, and ammunition hoists. Although destroyers of the 692 class were built from the same basic drawings, each construction yard had had its own ideas on installing pipes, ducts, and wiring. One day a foreman, asked to move another pipe, said wearily, "There isn't a pipe or a duct on this ship that hasn't been moved at least twice!"

Nevertheless, the destroyer *Meredith* came through with flying colors. Undoubtedly the greatest improvement was in the crew's mess. A dumbwaiter was installed to bring food from near the galley to the steam table, eliminating the perilous trip down the steep ladder and the prospect of the food getting cold en route. And instead of each crew member emptying his leavings into an open can, a mess attendant now scrapes the returned trays into a mechanical garbage disposal. Not only that, the long, regimented tables and the backless benches in the messroom have been replaced by tables for two and four, with seats having backs cushioned with foam rubber.

By arrangement, we gained room for a piano. There was some doubt whether the piano was worth its space and weight as a morale builder, but the captain assured a questioner that it was. However, when asked how many of the crew could play, he replied pointedly, "Three, including one who shouldn't."

CHAPTER 12. THE

A COMPETENT auto mechanic, confronted with a car that runs sluggishly, will in time locate the trouble and tune up the engine or, if necessary, overhaul it. One by one he will check the wiring, the ignition, the carburetor, the fuel pump, the coil. He has the knowledge and the experience and the tools for the job, and even if some unforeseen element, such as a corroded terminal on the battery, is at fault, he will eventually detect it. Similarly, the industrial designer has a *modus operandi*. No matter how elusive his assignment may be, he approaches it with confidence.

We have a yardstick in our office for good industrial design. It represents twenty-five years of experience, and we apply it to every design problem. It has five points:

1. UTILITY AND SAFETY.
2. MAINTENANCE.
3. COST.
4. SALES APPEAL.
5. APPEARANCE.

Other industrial designers may not state these points exactly as we do, but they are an essential part of the whole profession. Let us consider them in detail.

160

FIVE-POINT FORMULA

1. UTILITY AND SAFETY.   Is the automobile easy to handle? Does the vacuum cleaner roll lightly and smoothly over the rug? Is the telephone grip comfortable? Is the turn-off switch easy to find when the alarm clock rings? Are the complicated controls of an airplane easy for the pilot to identify? When we worked on the Mergenthaler linotype machine we made certain the controls were within easy reach. For a Link Aviation testing device we spent a great deal of time insuring quick legibility. On the Mosler bank-vault door we were concerned with the legibility of the combination dial.

Safety is a natural corollary to utility. Workers used to get badly injured on machinery. Today most hazards have been eliminated. On a Davidson duplicating machine the gear-drive mechanism was shrouded so that the operator's hands and clothing would not get caught in it. On a Warner and Swasey lathe various colored knobs to denote emergency controls were installed. The hydraulic control levers on National Supply's T 20 oil-drilling rigs were placed within easy reach for emergency use. Trade-unions have been a great factor in promoting safety, and we frequently key our work to patterns they have developed.

see page (50)

2. Maintenance. How easy is it to wash a milk bottle or a frying pan? Can you find the elusive places to oil a sewing machine or an electric shaver? How accessible are the cylinders on a Diesel or the engines on a transport plane or the gear chains of a farm implement? Maintenance must be an obvious thing. It must be easy to empty the grounds in a coffee maker or clean a plumbing fixture. The faucet handles on a Crane lavatory were mounted on ceramic pads so that housewives could wipe around them and not have to dig into nasty cracks. The forms of an Ingraham clock and an RCA television set are very simple and easy to clean. The cover of the new small, round Honeywell thermostat snaps off easily for quick access and maintenance of the interior apparatus. On the *New York Times* Stenofax duplicating machine the relays and working apparatus are on pull-out file-drawer panels so that the repairman can get to them easily. We often use carpet instead of linoleum because in many instances it is cheaper to clean over the years than to polish linoleum.

see page (51)

When our office undertook the ship interiors for the American Export liners *Constitution* and *Independence,* president John Slater cautioned, "Watch out for maintenance." A drastic instance soon confronted us. Before World War II, stewards remained on duty twenty-four hours a day, with only cat naps, and rested at the end of the voyage. Under a revision of working conditions, they went on eight-hour shifts. This meant that, if the Export Line was to continue full-time personal service, three times as many stewards would have to be fed, provided with sleeping quarters, and

162

cared for in foreign ports, a considerable added maintenance expense. The solution was found by revising the housekeeping system for passenger quarters. Passenger-operated beds, which slipped into position for sleeping when a foot pedal was pressed, were installed. Through such innovations, a full complement of stewards on night duty became unnecessary, and the line was able to provide better maintenance and service with fewer people.

3. COST. No matter how preoccupied the industrial designer is with the details of a new design, he is ever conscious of cost of manufacture and distribution. Even when it is not the overriding factor with the client, the designer tries to bring in a product under the estimate. There are two phases of cost of manufacture—tool costs and production costs. In items reproduced in comparatively small numbers, tooling costs are vital, as they must be prorated over small production. In the design of many mass-produced items, however, contemplated production is so large that the manufacturer can comfortably write off tooling costs. In either case, it is important to avoid increased production costs that are a continuing expense. The industrial designer recommends additional tooling if, by doing so, production costs will be appreciably reduced. In the long run, on the production lines, an article made in one piece instead of two or three saves a great deal in assembly. Take, for example, the cabinet of a table radio, which formerly was an assembly of many pieces of wood, each laboriously individually shaped, sanded, glued together, and finished; today the cabinet is the result of a single molding process using a

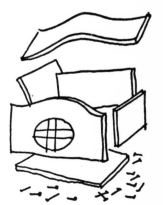

163

plastic compound. The cost of the mold necessary for this method of fabrication was more than offset by the savings on the assembly line.

The size of a product is also watched because by keeping it a quarter inch or a half inch smaller than originally planned, it is often found that more of them can be placed on a conveyor belt. The size and weight of a product also are important factors in cost of distribution.

4. SALES APPEAL. Many persons think sales appeal and appearance are synonymous, but they are not. Sales appeal is an elusive, psychological value. It is the subtle, silent selling the product must do, over and above its eye appeal. The product must express quality through unity of design, through texture, through simplicity and forthrightness. Soundlessly, it proclaims the excellence of its concealed mechanism and the integrity of its manufacturer. Sales appeal, therefore, is an amalgam of how a product feels to the touch, how it operates, and the association of pleasant ideas it conjures up in the purchaser's mind.

5. APPEARANCE. What does the product look like? Will a customer who sees it on a shelf in a store with half a dozen competing products single it out because of its appearance? Will it be remembered by the consumer who has briefly glimpsed it on TV or in a magazine ad? It is our experience that faithful application of the first four points of this yardstick give the product nine tenths of this appearance factor. The other tenth springs from the application of all we know of form, proportion, line, and color. Appearance is the common denominator. The whole emerges with

vitality and with the assurance required in the highly competitive market place.

In our office, these five points are accepted as infallible. We apply them unhesitatingly to a clock or an ocean liner, a turret lathe or a telephone, a tractor or a bathtub. To illustrate, let's relate them to a modern vacuum cleaner.

1. *Utility and safety of a vacuum cleaner.* To make an upright cleaner push and pull as comfortably as possible, we consider the length of the handle with relation to the specifications of Joe and Josephine and resolve the details of the handle grip to fit the hand. The position of the foot controls—the power switch and the nozzle adjustment—come in for scrutiny. The placement of the headlight to facilitate the viewing of dark areas must be determined. The height must be kept to a minimum, so that the cleaner will slide under low furniture. A rubber bumper protects walls and furnishings. Suitable handgrips for carrying the cleaner from one place to another are necessary. The size must be such that the cleaner can be conveniently stored in minimum closet space. The cleaning tools must be easy to attach. The electric cord must not kink, even when coiled. For safety's sake, the cleaner must have no sharp corners. The carton in which it is packed must serve a dual purpose—shipping and storage; likewise, the rack that holds the cleaning tools in shipment should be of a type that makes them easily accessible and orderly.

2. *Maintenance of a vacuum cleaner.* The disposable paper bag must be easily removable and the clean one put in place without effort. Incidentally, the removal of dirt from the

165

old cloth bag was one of the housewife's most hated tasks. The outside surface of the cleaner, whether plastic or enamel, must be easy to clean. The motor and other parts of the mechanism and the headlight bulb should be reachable without difficulty when replacements are needed.

③ *Cost of manufacture of a vacuum cleaner.* A careful study is made of materials. Factory assembly methods are examined. Savings can be effected by incorporating the motor housing and main casting in one piece; by simplifying the name-plate and the method of attaching it; in the fabrication of the bag; and in the selection of an enamel that covers in one coat instead of three.

④ *Sales appeal of a vacuum cleaner.* At first glance, some quality inherent in its contours rings a bell, exciting pleas-

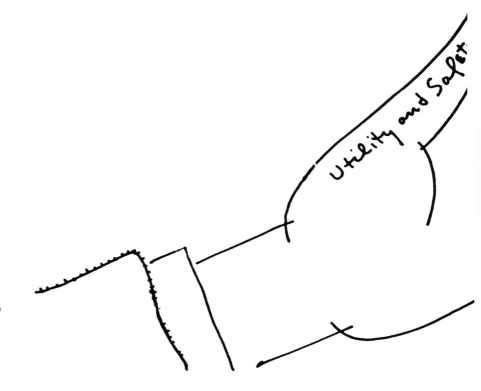

Utility and Safety

ant associations, evoking a confidence in the efficiency of the interior mechanism. The cleaner conveys the feeling that it is easy to push, light, balanced, and that the living room can be cleaned without awakening the old ache in the shoulder.

(5.) *Appearance of a vacuum cleaner.* Here the industrial designer adds the tangibles from his store of knowledge. These things are the end product of the designer's instinct, experience, and good taste. The cleaner is made pleasing to the eye by integration of line, proportion, form, color, and texture.

Thus, guided by the five-point formula, we are able to change what used to be the ugly duckling of the broom closet into a cleaner with clean, efficient, and functional lines.

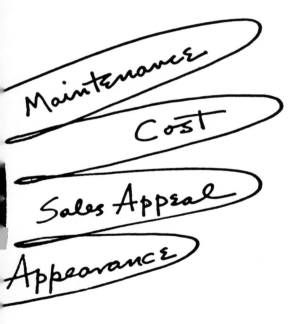

CHAPTER 13. RELATIONSHIP

ONCE a business executive has decided to employ an industrial designer, he may find himself in a dilemma. Which one should he select?

It is likely that he has read and heard about several of them or observed their performance in other industries. This may or may not help. Having had no previous dealings with any of them, the executive may be at a loss to appraise their work or to determine which of them is best qualified to do the job he has in mind. Backstage factors can be as important as those which are apparent. He may make the mistake of evaluating an industrial designer on the basis of a certain product, although the product may have been manufactured at calamitous cost or failed to receive public acceptance.

Then there is the matter of the fee. In a preliminary discussion with a manufacturer, I explained we did no work on speculation. He said, "That's like buying a pig in a poke." While mildly resenting the comparison, I have never forgotten the remark. It gave me a new appreciation of the manufacturer's quandary.

OF DESIGNER TO CLIENT

THERE are certain things the manufacturer should look for in making a final choice. The designer should have an understanding of the client's problem. He should know what the public wants and be familiar with merchandising methods. He should have knowledge of manufacturing and production methods and labor relations. He must know how to meet a schedule. He should be willing and able to cooperate with the employer's personnel and be sympathetic toward any insurmountable production limitations that might arise. And it can be presumed, of course, that along with all this goes the industrial designer's talent as an artist and his understanding of form, line, proportion, color, and texture.

If he can, the business executive should resist the impulse to make what has become almost an inevitable remark, "Of course, our product is different from any you've ever tackled." This may be true, but an industrial designer's work, by its very nature, is one of continually approaching and solving new problems. Moreover, the techniques he develops in working out a variety of problems qualify him

169

to come to grips with each one that is "different." What the business executive is looking for is a man of vision who is not a visionary, a practical merchant who is something of an artist, a fellow who lives in an ivory tower but has one foot on the ground, a personable diplomat who is equally at home in a high-level conference with the president and in a technical discussion with the operator of an eight-thousand-ton press. Curiously enough, that's just about what he gets.

ONCE he is selected, the industrial designer's primary responsibility, as in any profession, is to give the client value received. Ethically, he assumes other responsibilities, too, responsibilities far beyond the mere written agreement to help create or modify a certain article for a certain fee.

Suppose, on appraising the product on which he has been asked to work, he finds it is not feasible to proceed. Perhaps the product has not been properly tested, perhaps the material designated has not been proved. The industrial designer is obligated to protect the client, or the potential client, by pointing out that it would be a waste of money to put him on the job too soon.

Again, suppose the industrial designer finds, on inspecting the product, that the client expects more from him than it is in his power to deliver. The ethical designer will quickly explain that industrial design is not a cure-all for an ailing business.

It is understood, of course, that the industrial designer will take no competitive accounts, that he will keep confidential the nature of the work, and that he will do nothing that may react unfavorably to the design problem he has undertaken.

170

In his own behalf, he must insist on the authority to follow through his design from inception through production. In some instances, a manufacturer who has not worked before with an industrial designer may want to disregard his advice after the presentation stage and modify the design according to his own and his engineers' preferences. This is a shortsighted policy and, if it doesn't do worse damage, will at least waste the design investment.

The industrial designer is usually hired at the top level, that is, by the president, chief engineer, or sales manager of a firm. However, it is advisable that, once the preliminaries are over, the designer hasten to establish friendly working relations with the other departments, operating as a member of the organization, yet maintaining a diplomatic, professional perspective. At the risk of repeating, the importance of gaining the confidence and co-operation of the management, production, engineering, sales, advertising, and public-relations departments cannot be stressed too strongly. Without them, even if the "right" design is achieved, the product cannot be completely understood and therefore merchandised as enthusiastically as it might be.

UNTIL now, this discussion has dealt entirely with independent designers who have their own staffs. These may range in size from several hundred men to a single person. The services of the independent designer are, of course, available on the open market. There is another kind of designer, the corporate or internal designer, who is employed full time by a manufacturer and works on the manufacturer's premises.

Economically, it may seem advisable for a large corporation with a constant volume of design work to set up its own
design department. Whether the economics are sound over a
long period of time remains a question. There is the danger
that the internal designer, no matter how good he is, may
become frustrated by office politics and dulled by the sameness of his work, so that in time he loses his eagerness and his
originality and takes the easy way. When this happens, he
no longer creates; he is a captive.

Corporate design departments are especially useful in
plants where the material is basic and intimacy with it
essential, as in a glass factory. This is also true in big
organizations like Sears Roebuck and General Electric,
which turn out a great diversity of products. Even so, these
organizations will occasionally retain an independent designer for a particular product or line of products, believing
that his outside point of view will stimulate the staff
designers.

On big problems, industrial design can perhaps be best
executed by a collaboration between an outside consulting
organization and an internal liaison design group. In this
manner, the independent designer can bring to bear his
broad experience and diversified talents and the corporate
group can facilitate the application of their combined thinking. Unquestionably, the independent industrial designer
working on a wide diversity of products, in many factories,
acquires a knowledge of techniques, skills, cost-saving ideas,
new materials, and methods of fabrication that is almost
impossible for the internal designer to acquire. Besides, he
brings to a job an unrestricted point of view that cannot be

found confined within the same four walls day after day. Industrialists are becoming increasingly aware of the value of this outside point of view.

One of our clients once expressed this awareness when he said, "You are in effect an outsider looking over our shoulder as we work. I would say that this stimulates us to our best effort in our own design work. What's more, acceptance of a design, submitted by a recognized authority outside the company, is facilitated because of the very fact that it represents the opinion of someone not in our own ranks. In other words, we think you help us sell *our* ideas along with *your* ideas to our own people, and this can be a valuable asset."

Another facet of management's growing recognition of the importance of perspective is the fact that many of our clients maintain two distinct engineering groups, often geographically separated by being housed in separate buildings. One group concerns itself exclusively with the immediate problem of tooling up for tomorrow's product and getting it fitted into the production line. The other group is engrossed with problems farther over the horizon, decisions involving day *after* tomorrow's model. Necessarily, the industrial designer must work closely with both groups, developing future designs with one and helping the other guard the details of an accepted design as it goes through the tortures of tooling and mass production.

SOME persons think the industrial designer is the equivalent of a wonder drug like penicillin, to be used when sickness strikes. Actually, we are preventive medicine. Our long-time clients know this. Many of them have retained us year after year, in the manner of the old Chinese custom of paying a doctor a substantial fee once a year to keep the family well all year round. If it's an old-time client whose product isn't selling, we try to help; if it's a new client, we try to explain that a quick shot of vitamins is not the answer to his trouble, that his product probably needs a complete physical checkup.

During World War II, the then president of the Crane Company informed me that he wanted to cancel our agreement for the duration of the war. He added that he wanted to pay an honorarium so that we wouldn't work for anyone else in his field. I told him that because of existing conditions he didn't have to pay us and we wouldn't work for anyone else. He insisted and left a check. Three months later, he came to us and said he'd been wrong in canceling the agreement. "I want you to keep us up to date," he said. "I want you to be thinking of what we are going to make the day the war is over." He made available an entire floor of their building in Chicago, and we studied the Crane plumbing line item by item. Together we selected what should remain in the catalogue. Then we went to work designing new equipment to fill in the blank spaces. Metal was unobtainable except on priority, so full-size wooden models were built and enameled to simulate the actual porcelain. By the end of hostilities, Crane's postwar line of products was in readiness for manufacture. Thanks to the company's foresight, it gained a substantial time advantage in the market.

THE ideal relationship between client and independent industrial designer is one of friendly but respectful integration. Not long ago our office achieved it. This letter came from the executive vice-president of a client company: "We are finishing a good year. Perhaps you know that it has been our practice during good years to give some extra compensation to various of our employees. We think you have developed a fine basis for working with us; therefore, we are very glad to hand you the enclosed check, which may be taken as an indication of our feeling that you are one of us." The check was for a four-figured sum, but even so it didn't compare with the priceless warmth it gave us at being accepted into a client organization.

CHAPTER 14. THAT

HOW MUCH does it cost to hire an industrial designer? The answer may seem evasive, but it is the only honest one: the cost depends on what services are required.

There are numerous formulas for establishing fees. I can give only a reflection of our own practices, based on twenty-five years of experience and observation.

On his part, the industrial designer offers time and exclusive services. The value of the time is determined by experience, past performance, and reputation.

The industrial designer sells a design service, not a tangible product. In other words, all drawings, blueprints, models, are prepared for the client merely to explain or clarify the design.

Even in the early, struggling days of the profession, industrial designers pretty successfully resisted working on speculation. Today the practice is strictly taboo among firms of any standing.

Several fee arrangements have become almost standard:

1. ANNUAL BASIS. Except in unusual circumstances, we prefer an annual agreement, which comes up for discussion of renewal at the end of nine months. This gives both client and industrial designer an opportunity to suggest

SORDID SUBJECT, MONEY

modifications, discuss problems that may have arisen during the period, and come to a final agreement in time to plan for the next year. Such an annual agreement usually covers a complete line of products.

Payment can be made in the form of a monthly retainer fee plus time and expense, or as a flat inclusive retainer, on an annual basis.

New clients sometimes are not too clear as to just what they get for the monthly retainer fee. This is not surprising, in view of the fact that this fee actually covers a wide range of intangibles.

Perhaps the easiest way to explain the retainer fee is to break it down into the factors it covers. These are:

a. Availability. This means that the organization must be on call not only for the planned design program of the client, but also for unexpected emergency jobs. In both categories the work frequently is under pressure and in inaccessible locations.

b. Attention. This service is best explained by the phrase, "We bear the client constantly in mind," which appeared in a simple agreement used by our office. A thought that comes in the middle of the night or that is provoked by a news item, by something that the industrial designer has seen or heard—which might add something if applied to the client's product—fits into this category. For example, while traveling in Europe, I saw a small silver matchbox with a cover like an old-fashioned rolltop desk. This sparked an idea for an adaptation, which was suggested to a client; he brought out a traveling clock with a similar cover for the face to avoid breakage.

c. *Responsibility.* The industrial designer's fee is often considered almost as extra insurance. His advice can sometimes literally mean business life or death to the client. This is a grave responsibility. The principal designer is usually held responsible for the work of the entire organization.

d. *Use of name.* The use of the industrial designer's name is usually limited by contract. Most designers will permit such use only when the final product has been approved by them. A designer's name is often a valuable asset, especially if he has a national reputation, and the prestige of his name will help sell the product.

e. *Exclusive services.* By this, the industrial designer assures the client that he will not work on a competitive product.

f. *Principal's time.* Most designers include this in the retainer fee. The alternative is to charge the principal's time on a straight hourly basis.

Other time costs are usually handled on a predetermined hourly rate for each designer, draftsman, modelmaker, or researcher. This rate includes a percentage to cover overhead and profit.

Out-of-pocket expenses are usually charged to the client

at cost plus a nominal overhead charge, except for such direct expenses as travel, which are on a net basis.

✓**2. FLAT INCLUSIVE RETAINER ON AN ANNUAL BASIS.** This can usually be arrived at only after the industrial designer has worked with a client over a considerable period, and the amount of time and work involved can be gauged. Some clients prefer a flat fee because they know what their design budget will be for the year. In many ways, this arrangement is most desirable for all concerned, because it eliminates the time-clock factor.

✓**3. SPECIFIC JOB.** This type of agreement is used when the client has a particular job to be done and there is reason to believe that when it has been completed no further industrial-design advice will be needed. The client in this category usually makes but one product and sticks to the same design over a period of years. Agreements of this kind specify a time limit and a flat all-inclusive fee.

✓**4. ROYALTY.** In this type of arrangement, the designer receives a percentage of the sales price of the article he has designed. It is used mostly in the furniture and home-furnishings fields. Although we have never worked on this basis, many designers have found it highly satisfactory.

OF these four types of arrangements, the annual retainers are preferred by most industrial designers. An annual arrangement is usually made when designer and client look forward to a long-term association, continued from year to year. In our office we derive great satisfaction from the general longevity of our client relationship—one of which dates back to 1930 and several to 1934 and 1935.

Contracts between industrial designer and client can range up to ten pages of fine print. In our case, we have not been successful in developing a typical contract, because almost every client's problems seem to require variations to fit his particular case. The agreement we use generally is one and a half typewritten pages long and is worded elastically so that the client is not limited in the services he is entitled to expect from us and we are not limited in the degree of co-operation we can expect from him. It was worked out without benefit of a lawyer, and we consider it merely a written explanation of an understanding rather than a legal document. It is our feeling that, if a client decided he no longer wanted to work with us, we would not want to hold him to a contract, and vice versa. No contract can control the quality of a creative service such as industrial design. We have never tried to tie anything down legally, and we have never had a lawsuit.

Some of our most important jobs have been done without a word on paper. We tried for almost a year, off and on, to work out a mutually acceptable agreement with *McCall's*, but the ones we presented were too vague to suit their legal department. The ones they sent us were too limiting to suit us. Nevertheless, we worked with them for twelve years. A similar situation existed with the New York Central System. The vice-president who hired us advised us not to attempt to write a contract, as the Central's legal department was very precise and would insist that we spell out exactly what we were going to give them for their money. To do this, we agreed, would limit our activity. During our long collaboration, the annual agreements between us were reached at yearly fifteen-minute meetings, where a hand-shake sealed our mutual understanding of our relationship for the coming twelve months.

Our philosophy of contracts is based on mutual respect and faith. The only purpose of the agreement is to clarify certain factors that experience has taught us might other-wise cause misunderstandings.

In practical terms, the designer's fee is an excellent insurance policy for the manufacturer to take out against the cost of his machine tools.

CHAPTER 15.

SOMETIMES there is no explanation for the things that happen to an industrial designer, except perhaps that the gremlins, leprechauns, and poltergeists are working overtime.

An example of what I am talking about happened in 1939, when the New York World's Fair was formally launched by President Franklin D. Roosevelt and all the people who worked on it were notified in advance by Grover Whalen that they would march in a procession to where F.D.R. presided over a court of honor. The last few hours before the opening of any fair are always chaotic, and this was no exception. When the time came for the procession to start, I was still in the Perisphere, working with paint and plaster. But as the trumpets sounded from the tops of the buildings I found my place in the ranks with my colleagues and felt impressed, indeed—until the loudspeaker announced the sequence of the marching groups. "The Comfort Station Attendants," it advised the world, "will be followed by the Industrial Designers."

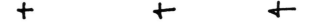

WE WERE engaged by W. K. Vanderbilt to do the interior of the large Sikorsky amphibious plane in which he later

NOT BY DESIGN

toured South America. It was designed to be self-sufficient, so it could fly into port each night and the passengers could eat and sleep aboard. It was luxuriously furnished with a kitchen, bedrooms, dressing rooms, shower, and a bar. The day the plane was ready for delivery, I went to Roosevelt Field, in New York, where it had been flown down from the factory in Bridgeport. Soon the Vanderbilts drove up in a large limousine. Mr. Vanderbilt climbed the ladder and disappeared into the hatch, located on top of the fuselage. He was followed by Mrs. Vanderbilt, noted for her addiction to enormous hats, one of which she was wearing. As she reached the hatch she stopped, looked around the hangar, motioned to me, and said, "My man, this door will have to be made larger." I introduced myself and suggested she take off her hat. She smiled graciously, removed it, and went down the hatch.

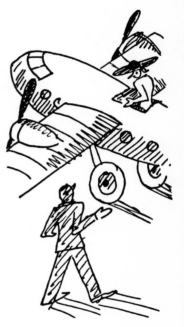

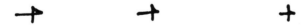

ONE OF the hundreds of the settings we did for the Radio-Keith-Orpheum circuit was a background for the act of a famous contortionist called Ferry the Frog Man. It was a woodland glen with oversize plants and leaves and an enormous toadstool that served as a pedestal for Ferry's gyrations. After the first performance, Ferry cornered me backstage and thanked me for the set. As an afterthought, he added seriously, "Mr. Dreyfuss, I wonder if you might find some use for my wife—she's a lizard, you know."

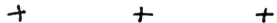

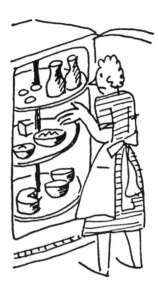

SIX YEARS ago, seeking a midnight snack as is my habit, I went foraging in the refrigerator. I was confronted with the usual forest of bottles and containers and, as always, the Cheddar cheese I wanted to put on some crackers was far in the back, out of reach. I resolved to do something about this intolerable situation. Why not revolving shelves? I prevailed upon our client, General Electric, to make a few experimental refrigerators with such shelves and, as a test, installed one in my kitchen alongside the one already there. At last my nightly dilemma was solved. I could open the refrigerator, spin the shelves, and find anything I wanted. It was like a filing cabinet. Elated, I asked the housekeeper how she liked the new revolving shelves. She looked at me blankly and said, "You use it, Mr. Dreyfuss. I'll use the other one." It seemed she had kept the butter in the same place on the same shelf for years, the eggs in another particular spot, the milk in another. She wanted to be able to go to the refrigerator and instinctively find what she was after. With the revolving refrigerator shelf she was unable to do this. GE was equally unenthusiastic. But this was half a dozen years ago. GE recently brought out an improvement on this revolving shelf, a semicircular arrangement that makes but half a turn and answered our housekeeper's objections.

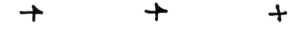

WHEN I worked in the theater, many years ago, an urgent need arose for some large, gold Chinese characters to be written on an atmospheric pagodalike setting we had constructed. I stopped at the public library and found some Chinese writing that looked quite decorative and reproduced it on the set. After the first performance I had a backstage visitor, a pleasant Chinese gentleman who had seen the show and who asked if I knew what was written on the scenery. I said I didn't. He informed me the characters translated meant, "Grandpa spanks the baby." It seemed I had consulted a Chinese primer.

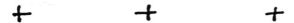

ANOTHER TIME at the Strand in New York, I worked out an atmospheric bit for an act called Gerry and Her Baby Grands, a four-piano team. Instead of having the four instruments placed all over the stage, I dreamed up the idea of a huge simulated piano encompassing the width of all four keyboards. It was finished just in time for the opening performance, at which point I discovered it was too big to move through the stage entrance. My boss was the famous showman, Joseph L. Plunkett, managing director of the theater. A man of less forbearance would have fired me on the spot, but Plunkett chalked it up to experience.

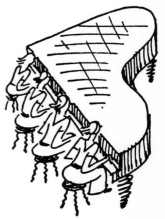

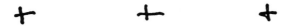

WE ONCE did a large diorama or mechanical model of a scene at Kitty Hawk for a Standard Oil exhibit at Radio City. At the opening, refreshments were served with a lavish hand. An executive of the company spoke briefly, explaining that it was a historical view of the Wright brothers at Kitty Hawk—only he called it Cutty Sark.

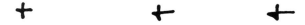

No ONE likes a puddle of coffee in his saucer. We were determined to correct this annoyance when we designed the table service for the New York Central System, and we molded a cup that sloped inward toward the top. This shape, we thought, would contain the liquid despite the turbulence of a moving train. The first trip was disastrous. The vibration of the train set up a harmonic action that caused the coffee to slosh all over the tablecloth. We reverted to straight-sided cups and relied on the old railroad tradition that an inverted spoon standing up in the cup cuts down on the spilling. Strangely enough, the identical inward-sloping cups proved spillproof when we tried them on the gently rolling S.S. *Independence*. But in a really rough sea, the best of designers is well advised to supply coffee drinkers with absorbent paper doilies to blot up the overflow.

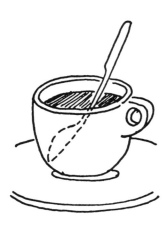

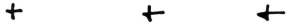

DURING the early period when I was designing scenery and costumes for the theater, I decided to learn how clothes were put together so that, when the occasion required, I could superintend the alteration of a badly fitted jacket or sleeve. I found that Columbia University gave an extension course in dressmaking, and I enrolled—to find myself in the company of seventy-one women. I remained untroubled by being outnumbered until it was announced that the examination problem would be for each student to cut and fit a dress for the occupant of the next seat. The day of the test I nervously entered the classroom. I quickly relaxed. Amid titters, I discovered my worktable had been provided with a headless, armless, and certainly sexless dressmaker's dummy.

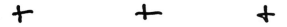

DURING the Chicago Fair, General Electric put on a show of its products. A kitchen was set up, and a voice on a sound track explained that it was the voice of General Electric and in turn described each unit. A bright spotlight focused on each unit being described. On opening night something went wrong with the mechanical system and the voice said, "I am a General Electric dishwasher," and the door of the electric stove's oven opened and the washing machine started. There were a frantic few moments before the machinery could be stopped and synchronized.

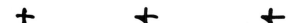

WHEN WE worked for the American Export ships, we designed some small glass ash trays with the Export insignia on them. They were quite handsome and distinctive, perhaps too much so. During the exhibition of the ships, more than three thousand of the ash trays disappeared. Many companies, by the way, deliberately encourage the removal of ash trays as souvenirs. They think it is good advertising to have them in people's homes.

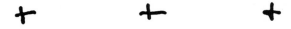

In our work at the New York World's Fair, we were under instructions to prepare an exhibit building for two years' use, and we considered materials that would wear well and not require repainting or other maintenance. We installed indestructible sheet rubber to cover the many columns. Soon we noticed that a curious efflorescence was appearing on the rubber. Everyone had forgotten that the Fair was built on a former city dump, and the decomposing materials gave off gasses that acted on the rubber. It was too late to do anything except accept the inevitable—and for two years the rubber received a daily wash.

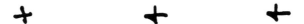

When we designed some railroad cars for the Budd Company, we discovered, just in time, that the emergency tool kits mounted in the front end of the coaches were useless. These were so placed that passengers, in the event of a wreck, might cut their way out. But they had been installed behind unbreakable safety glass. Someone had followed our specifications too closely.

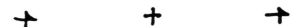

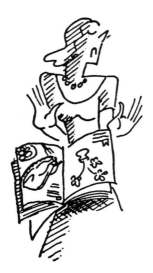

Many years ago, in our work on *McCall's Magazine*, we experimented with odors in inks, an idea some newspapers have since put into practice. My thought was that there would be great novelty in having the odor of a fine cut of beef, for instance, emanate from a page showing a luscious roast, and so on throughout the magazine. The experiment was noxious. The juxtaposition of soap and frying fish, perfume and disinfectants, condiments and cosmetics, turned out to be overpowering.

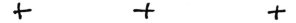

ONE OF OUR disappointments was a gray plastic handle for a lavatory. It seemed a good idea at the time, which was just after World War II. Unable to tool all the metal designs it wanted in time for the postwar business, and with chrome still at a premium, the Crane Company, at our suggestion, decided to try gray plastic. The handle failed miserably, for reasons best described as psychological. As a wartime measure, many articles in the plumbing line had been put out in unfinished gray iron. The color recalled to the public's mind the rough cast-iron handles they'd put up with unhappily during the war, and they refused to buy our new handle. Today plastics enjoy universal acceptance.

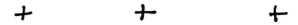

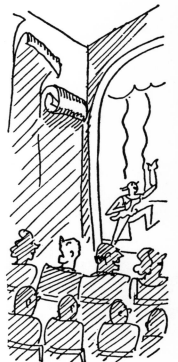

SOME YEARS AGO, in designing a new three-thousand-seat theater in Denver for Radio-Keith-Orpheum, we decided to use a new material, a thin veneer of real wood bonded to canvas, to cover the walls. On the gala opening night, as I sat next to the governor of Colorado, I looked around to inspect our handiwork. To my horror, the material was slowly unrolling down the sixty-foot walls. The material, unfortunately, had been put on a wet plaster wall. The damage was easily repaired, and the walls are still standing firm.

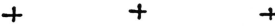

ONE OF OUR early jobs was doing over the Roseland dance hall. We brightened it by using mirrors all around the dance floor and behind the bandstand. The day before the opening, Julian Everett of our office went over and stood in the center of the dance floor for a final look, to make sure everything was all right. At that moment the door of the ladies' room opened, and the embarrassed Mr. Everett discovered that, owing to ricocheting mirror reflections, he could see things he wasn't supposed to see. A screen was hurriedly erected.

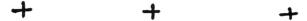

I HAD BEEN invited to speak before the Cleveland Advertising Club. Upon arriving, I was amazed at an audience numbering several thousand, and secretly flattered that they had come to hear an industrial designer. Luncheon over, the mayor of the city arose, and I took a last gulp of water and awaited the introduction. My glow faded when he introduced the local basketball team, which had won the championship and was there to receive an award. They were the real reason for the big crowd. I was low man on the totem pole. The pleasant ending of the story is that, after my talk, a stranger approached and asked if I could spare an hour to visit his factory. He was the late Clifford Stilwell, vice-president of Warner and Swasey. Before the day was over we were retained by his company. That was in 1939. We are still working for them.

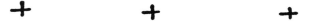

ZIPPERS, according to the U. S. patent office, were used during the Civil War, but they weren't discovered by me

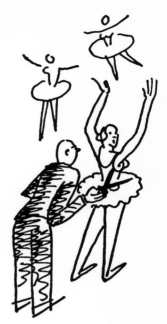

until about thirty years ago. This was during my early days at the Strand Theater. I used them on one occasion on the tight bodices of forty young ladies in the *corps de ballet*. All went well at the rehearsal, but during the opening performance, the dancers' overheated bodies caused the costumes to cling in a manner that made the zippers jam. A quick costume change was necessary, and, in a panic, we cut the girls out of their clothes with scissors.

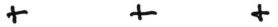

ONE TIME several representatives of a widely known museum called on me and said they would like to exhibit some of my designs. This seemed flattering. The museum had never put on a one-man industrial-design show. I brought out numerous sketches and models for them to inspect. One said doubtfully, "The numerals on this clock dial seem out of proportion." Another asked, "Why did you put that chrome on the bottom of the typewriter?" Rather than try to explain, I suggested that we forget the idea of an exhibit. It occurred to me that the only museums in which I care to show my work are places like Macy's, Marshall Field's, and the May Company, and I hope never to have a permanent exhibit in any of them. This was many years ago. Today, museums have embraced industrial design.

191

CHAPTER 16. WHY ARE

IN talks and panel discussions, I have found that a question period frequently prompts more rewarding information about industrial design than do prepared speeches. Over the years I have kept a record of the questions most frequently asked.

Q. *Why are barns painted red?*

A. Since this question is so often asked, I have done some checking, for I have always been fascinated by the simple beauty of these red barns. They were built, as almost everything should be, from the inside out. A farmer needed a place to keep his livestock and store his feed and tools. So a building took shape around these needs—four walls and a roof. Simple doors and windows were placed where they were needed, not to achieve exterior symmetry. This is functional architecture at its finest. But why are these barns painted red? Out of curiosity, I queried people who might know—artists, educators, architects, museum researchers, businessmen, designers, and farmers. Some of the answers that flowed in follow:

Architect Eero Saarinen expressed the belief that the

How will the development of atomic power affect industry?
How lasting are today's designs?
Can a small manufacturer afford an industrial designer?

BARNS PAINTED RED?

tradition of painting barns red originated in Finland and Sweden because red—"red earth"—was the only available paint. Financier Harry B. Lake and Faber Birren, the color expert, stated that barns were painted red, originally in New England, because the color absorbed the solar heat and insured a warmer barn for the livestock during the winter. Grandma Moses agrees that the practice started in New England but she believes that red barn paint originally was made by mixing linseed oil with a certain kind of clay which resembled decayed iron ore. The result, an inexpensive and lasting paint, was found to have no lead properties which could be poisonous to cows. Francis Henry Taylor, of the Metropolitan Museum of Art, dug up the fact that most paint preservatives are reddish, making it easiest to use them in red paint without destroying the color. On the other hand, William W. Wurster, dean of the School of Architecture at the University of California, said that the color red has no special durability factor since it is the oil that is important. Architect W. K. Harrison replied, "Red paint is cheap, covers well, and does not show dirt." This view was echoed by Advertising Man Leo Burnett and Scenic Designer Jo Mielziner, who added that red lead was

193

the best protection against the weather. Industrial Designer Harold Van Doren stated that he didn't know why, but he knew how farmers got their barns painted red—it was done free by the Mail Pouch Tobacco Company in return for advertising privileges. Similarly, Architect Ralph Walker expressed the opinion that barns were painted red to give a background to ads for Carter's Little Liver Pills. William Otto, executive of the Pittsburgh Plate Glass Company, which manufactures paint as well as glass, said that the red paint used on barns in bygone days derived from Venetian red—an economical, durable paintmaker's pigment still utilized in low-cost barn paints. He pointed out that it is an earth color, as opposed to chemically derived colors, and has more permanency than the chemical varieties. Industrial Designer Egmont Arens stated that the prosperity of farms in Iowa used to be judged by the color of their barns— white in good times and red in hard times. Business Counselor Sheldon Coons suggested that the reason was that red stood out so well against snow on Christmas cards.

I prefer to believe that farmers of an earlier day felt, as we do today, that when the landscape is blanketed with snow, red barns give a feeling of warmth and security. And so a tradition grew.

Q. *Can a small manufacturer afford an industrial designer?*

A. He cannot afford to be without one, because industrial design is a great equalizer. The public isn't interested in the size of the manufacturer; it is interested only in getting its money's worth. In other words, a small manufacturer's product must compete in the open market with the big manufacturer's product. Suppose ten men pool their funds and make an electric toaster—a good electric toaster—and put it on the market. Their product is still going to have to stand comparison with General Electric and Toastmaster. If the small manufacturer is going to meet them on even terms, he will be wise to buy a share in the time of a competent industrial designer. It may come high, but he buys all the designer's experience with his fee.

Q. *How do you become an industrial designer?*

A. Today's industrial designers are mostly created in industrial-design offices. Many are educated architects or engineers. Some are self-trained. Some are from art schools. Architecture and engineering give excellent background for industrial design because they teach people to think in an orderly fashion and in three dimensions. Some art schools that give industrial-design courses are good, but others turn out people who can make a handsome rendering or a well-finished model that couldn't possibly be translated into a satisfactory product. Our goal is more college courses in industrial design, terminating in a degree. Such graduates would be prepared to measure public taste, understand production problems, comprehend a budget and balance sheet, talk business on an executive level with a client, be salesmen, diplomats, psychologists, and be able to work intelligently with engineers. In order to conceive future designs, they should have a talking knowledge of the history of art and architecture. It is an imposing combination, but

195

if a student can get the beginnings of it in the universities, he will be on his way. And universities are becoming increasingly cognizant of industrial design.

Q. *Has modern technology reached its peak; in other words, has it outstripped the capacity of people to assimilate its benefits?*

A. The best answer to this question is to be found in the *Patent Office Society Journal.* A man named Eber Jeffery did some research in 1940 on a quotation attributed to a Patent Office employee who quit his job a century ago, saying, " Opportunity is dead! All possible inventions have been invented. All great discoveries have been made." Jeffery was unable to establish the identity of the disheartened employee, but he uncovered several other versions of the statement. A discouraged examiner was said to have stated in his letter of resignation that there was no future for the inventor. A Congressman favoring the elimination of the Patent Office stated that the time was near when its functions would serve no purpose. Most likely the quotation derived from Commissioner of Patents Henry Ellsworth, who resigned in April, 1845. He is supposed to have given as his reason that the limits of human ingenuity already had been reached, but this was not substantiated. However, he did state in a report to Congress in 1843, "The advancement of the arts from year to year taxes our credulity and seems to presage the arrival of that period when human improvement must end."

Remember, this was a century ago, before the invention of the electric light, the automobile, the radio, the airplane.

Q. *How will the development of atomic power affect industry?*

A. A clue to the answer lies in the fact that many big concerns already are looking ahead to the time that this new source of power comes into common use. American Machine and Foundry has developed a nuclear power plant, designed for use in remote areas, that would operate for three years without refueling. At the end of three years, the plant could be completely refueled by one flight of one airplane. This plant would deliver approximately one thousand kilowatts, sufficient to furnish electrification to a residential community of around one thousand homes. To supply the same amount of power for the same period, a coal-powered plant would require 10,200,000 pounds, or 75 carloads, of fuel, an oil-powered plant would need 4,266,000 pounds, or 69 carloads, of oil. We are on the brink of a new era in efficiently and inexpensively produced power.

Q. *Is packaging a part of industrial design?*

A. Yes, a very important part. Some industrial designers do packaging exclusively. Some large offices have special departments for it. Packaging has become a vital part of modern business. Watch the procession of carts at the checkout counter of a busy supermarket. The colorful array of packaging is evidence of the know-how of the packaging expert. He has helped persuade the shopper to select one item over another, although they may be identical in purpose, quality, and price. More subtle packaging may be found on the shelves of the drugstore. The paradox is reached, of course, at the cosmetic counter, where the vial is often more costly than the contents.

There is much more to packaging, naturally, than what is visual. Long before cartons and bottles were eye-arresting, they were necessary as containers and as protection. This is still true. The packaging specialist must be completely familiar with materials—kraftboard, wooden barrels, tin cans, plastic, paper, glass, cellophane, and the new synthetic coatings. A plastic coating for dill pickles, to be peeled off when ready for eating, is now successfully being marketed. The plastic squeeze bottle for liquids has become almost universal.

The packaging expert must know what will stand up best in shipping; what excessive heat and cold will do to the product and how to insulate against it; he must understand the problem of weight and know what fastenings the post office and express companies demand for shipment. He must be aware that a great deal of merchandise goes air freight—often needing less protection because of careful handling but also requiring lightweight containers. The package designer must be an expert in typography and must test legibility in the various degrees of illumination where the product will be sold. He must understand inks and printing and labeling. He should be alert to colors that will fade in the bright sunshine of a display window, lest the merchandise seem shopworn and therefore unsalable. He must understand the processes of packaging machinery. The carton or wrapper is sometimes closed around the can or bottle at lightning speed, and the package must be designed to facilitate, not hinder, the pace of sixty-five loaves of bread being wrapped in a minute, one hundred and fifty packages of cigarettes, six hundred sticks of gum, or the filling and capping of two hundred and forty Coca-Cola bottles.

Equally important, the package expresses the quality of its contents. It would be difficult for the shopper to know the difference between one flour or rice or coffee and another, but she recognizes an advertised package and, once she has used and approved the contents, will return to buy it again.

Products other than foods and drugs are carefully packaged. Vacuum cleaners, clocks, utilities of all kinds, come in boxes that must be protective and attractive. Tennis balls come in airtight cans and watches in molded plastic cases. Spare parts for heavy-machinery components of farm implements, oil-well-drilling machinery, Diesel engines, pumps, all come protected in carefully designed cartons and wrappings. It has proved to be good merchandising to pack eight spark plugs to a box and thus sell a complete replacement. The six sides of a box or the circumference of a can provide excellent advertising display. From the quart of oil at a service station to a stick of gum in the drugstore, there is no better place to sell the virtues of a product than on its own jacket. The selling need not be done in so many words as in the atmosphere or identification created by the picture or design or color combinations.

Q. *What is the dividing line between industrial design and architecture?*

A. Many of us think the two get closer every year. There is no question that the industrial designer has contributed a great deal to architecture, particularly in relation to store interiors, theaters, gasoline service stations, and display buildings. On assignments of this kind, the industrial designer utilizes his study of the mass mind and the mass market and his experience in merchandising generally, translating them into stone, steel, and plaster. If he can produce a background that invites customers to stop and shop and buy, he has given the building meaning.

Industrial designers have been outstandingly successful at fairs and exhibitions, where the temporary nature of the buildings permits experimentation in architecture and produces ideas that often prove acceptable in future permanent structures. Recall the tremendous interest created by Norman Bel Geddes' General Motors show at the New York World's Fair.

I have always felt that the industrial designer is ideally suited to design a prefabricated house. His knowledge of consumer demands, his understanding of research, his ability to apply functionalism as well as beauty, his background in factory techniques, and his grasp of costs equip him to tackle this type of assembly-line operation. A person gets less for his money when he custom-builds a house than in any other major expenditure. If we ordered our automobiles custom-made as we do our houses, the cost of one Chevrolet would be staggering. Mass production of houses would alleviate this condition.

My one experience with a prefab house was disappointing. In 1945, shortly before the end of World War II, Consolidated Vultee, for whom we had worked on airplanes, decided to enter this field, to keep their vast plants busy, and asked us to prepare a design. Many millions of dollars were spent to produce the finished product, just as a fortune is required to roll the first new Chevvie out of Detroit. It was completely acceptable. The critical FHA believed that it would solve the desperate housing problem. The company went ahead on a schedule calling for twenty finished houses a day. But the bad luck that seems to pursue prefabrication followed us. Eventually, Consolidated Vultee directors decided that the building business, with its local labor problems and local building codes, was too involved to deal with and abandoned the project. A few of the experimental houses may still be seen around the countryside, and I find myself wistfully gazing at them whenever I pass by.

Q. *How do you start an industrial-design problem?*

A. We begin with men and women and we end with them. We consider the potential users' habits, physical dimensions, and psychological impulses. We also measure their purse, which is what I meant by ending with them, for we must conceive not only a satisfactory design, but also one that incorporates that indefinable appeal to assure purchase. The Greek philosopher Protagoras had a phrase for it, "Man is the measure of all things."

Q. *How do you prevent plagiarism of your designs?*

A. Many of our designs are patented and assigned to our clients, but designs, like ideas, are difficult to protect. There is no accounting for coincidence of ideas. Often a

201

design is conceived behind locked doors and kept in utmost secrecy all through production. Yet, just before or simultaneously with its appearance on the market, a competitor will release an almost identical design.

We do not believe that honest manufacturers willfully plagiarize each other's designs. I have heard Archibald MacLeish hold forth on similar coincidences that occur in literature, poetry, and music. My own belief is that the things happening around us act as stimuli to people in widely separated places. They create an atmosphere or climate that produces identical ideas. The influence of a jet plane, a new variety of flower, music, a superbomb, a meeting of powerful rulers, a romantic love match, change of seasons, a great painting, a comic strip—all these certainly suggest different things to different people. The coincidence occurs when two people are influenced in the same way at the same time and produce similar results.

Q. *Is good taste inherent or acquired?*

A. A few persons seem to be born with the gift of selection, as a fortunate few are endowed from birth with the talent to sing in opera or to paint fine pictures or to write first-rate plays. But for most people, the ability to select things in good taste is cultivated.

Some have a head start by being exposed from childhood to fine surroundings or through the influence of discriminating families or associates. Others acquire good taste from study and practice, with a resultant growing appreciation.

Others turn to objects of tasteful appearance in revolt from long exposure to bad taste.

Not too many years ago it was difficult for persons in low-income brackets or in isolated places to develop this judgment. Everyday objects in good form and good color were not generally available.

Today manufacturers and merchandisers, prodded gently by the industrial designer, have learned that well-designed products need cost no more than poorly designed ones and are more acceptable to the come-of-age consumer.

What all this proves is that most people have a feeling for good taste but that it is likely to be latent and needs to be awakened, stimulated, and developed. The industrial designer plays a leading role in this awakening.

Q. *I am in my thirties. Is it too late for me to become an industrial designer?*

A. Age is only relative to the individual. Gauguin was thirty-five years old before he really started painting. Michelangelo was seventy-two when he was called upon to design St. Peter's.

Assuming that you have had some art, architecture, or engineering training and that you are convinced of your good taste, try this exercise. Walk through a department store or carefully examine a mail-order catalogue or just look around your own home. Select a dozen items that do not suit your fancy and seriously study them, then make an attempt to redesign them. Do not limit yourself to their appearance; apply the five rules set down on page 160 of this book.

203

When you have finished, ask a practicing industrial designer to evaluate the result.

Q. *What is the SID?*

A. The initials are those of the Society of Industrial Designers, an organization I am proud to have helped organize. It grew out of a casual week-end discussion with Walter Dorwin Teague in 1944. We talked of the advisability of an organization that would keep the ethics of this growing profession on a high plane and foster the education of future industrial designers. The next day, in New York, we outlined the idea to Raymond Loewy. We agreed on the feasibility of such an organization, and each invited seven other designers to join us. Thus, the SID was born. Since its inception, the Society's strict code of ethics has done much to give dignity to the profession.

Membership, now one hundred and sixty-nine, is limited through high qualifications. Five chapters divide the country geographically, and each holds separate meetings in which new ideas are initiated and decisions of the national office and its board of directors are carried out. The annual meeting attracts members from all over the United States and Canada.

A spirit of friendliness is apparent throughout the SID. Members consider themselves colleagues with a common goal rather than competitors. They have an awareness of their influence upon the taste of so many millions of people and a feeling of responsibility. They lecture all over the world, spreading the true doctrine of the profession. They are constantly invited to speak at universities, museums, civic organizations, and service clubs.

There is another organization of designers in this country called the Industrial Designers' Institute. The SID and the IDI are not to be considered as competitive. In some few instances, designers hold memberships in both organizations. The two groups occasionally confer on matters of common interest, explore situations that affect their membership, and often act jointly in presenting a solid front—to the satisfaction of SID and IDI members and sometimes the surprise of the public.

Q. *Are you bothered much by people who think they have a great design idea?*

A. I can only assume that other industrial designers are beset, as I am, at dinner parties, in theater lobbies, on the street, or while strapped in an airplane seat, by enthusiastic souls, usually females, who have what they consider world-shaking suggestions. These suggestions vary from kitchen gadgetry to a contrivance for a guided missile, and they are almost always accompanied by an offhand remark about being included in the fantastic profits that will inevitably result.

Poor, polite souls that we are, we listen intently. Such listening is hazardous. There is always the danger that by coincidence the suggested idea is already being developed by a client or ourselves and it is good sense to avoid the possible threat of a lawsuit for "stealing" an idea.

More than likely the suggested idea is not original and

we are faced with the unpleasant duty of advising the person that this is the case. The incredulous, icy stare that follows is hardly thanks for our honesty.

Q. *How lasting are today's designs?*

A. Sometimes, to dramatize the fact that the modern products of industry are made more efficient, more functional, and more eye-appealing by industrial design, designers like to show "before" and "after" pictures—comparing today's sleek gas range, for instance, with the black cast-iron kitchen stove Grandmother used. I have found that this seemingly harmless bit of showmanship can backfire. In the minds of some people it creates the impression that the industrial designer is so fatuous as to believe that his work, unlike Grandmother's stove, never will become outdated. Actually, the industrial designer believes no such thing. The fact is that people and people's taste change, making today's design obsolete tomorrow. This kind of obsolescence can be an important sales factor in certain types of nondurable merchandise and sometimes is deliberately accelerated by design. Also, technological advances in this swift-moving world often combine to outdate the best of designs. The pull-chain toilet, for instance, was a fine example of functionalism. So were and still are the broom and the carpet sweeper. Engineering, electronic, and mechanical developments have made them almost as old-fashioned as the one-horse shay. By this I do not mean to imply that the conscientious designer isn't striving for longevity in his designs. He strives to make his modern designs as "classical" as possible, in the hope that they will live. But we designers are realists. We are keenly aware of the attrition of changing public taste and relentlessly advancing technology. I try always to keep the sobering thought in mind that everything was modern the day it was created. When I hear a designer laugh at a piece of Victorian furniture, I am tempted to say, "Careful, now! Are you sure people won't be laughing at your furniture a hundred years from now?" And, finally, to keep things in focus, I like to imagine the Grecian shepherd who came down from the hills one day and viewed for the first time the newly completed Parthenon and said, "I *hate* modern architecture!"

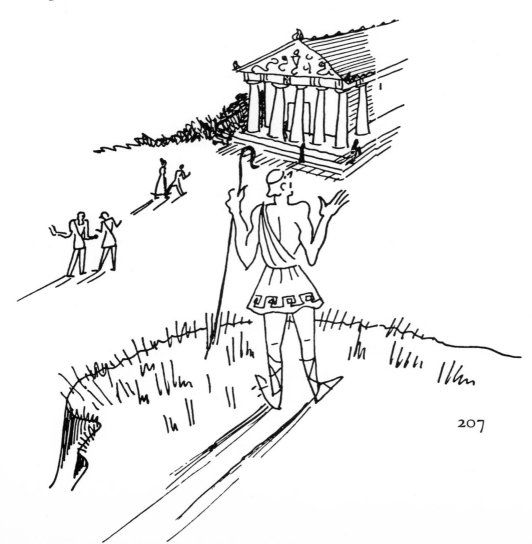

207

CHAPTER 17. PROFILE

WHAT makes an industrial-design organization tick? How does it operate?

These are fair questions and frequently asked of the independent designer. But, like many fair questions, they are difficult to generalize upon. The reason is that there is no universal *modus operandi* among designers. Walter Dorwin Teague, Raymond Loewy, Harold Van Doren, David Chapman, Hunt Lewis, and Jean Reinecke are all successful practitioners in the field, yet their organizations range in size from one man to hundreds; their methods are as varied as their personalities.

Thus, when I answer these questions by describing my own organization it is not that it is typical, but that it is the only one on which I am qualified to speak.

I OPENED my first industrial-design office in 1929. It was the time of the stock-market crash and the most catastrophic business and financial collapse in history. My new venture, an unknown and experimental profession headed by an unknown and experimenting designer, seemed to have little chance to survive. It would have been prudent, perhaps, to close the office and let the storm pass. But there was also the long-shot possibility that such a "depression baby"

OF AN ORGANIZATION

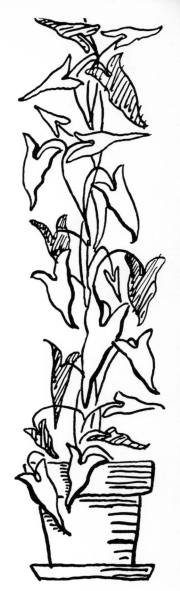

might make it. Industry was in trouble, and businessmen, caught in a hectic scramble to sell their static merchandise, might come to us for design advice.

The day I opened the office, I felt the urge to make some commemorative gesture. I bought a small potted plant for twenty-five cents. The plant originally had two pathetic green leaves, but it turned out to be a living lucky piece. Twenty-five years and several moves later, it stands today in our office, luxuriant and ceiling-high. In a limited circle, it has become rather famous. As often as not, old clients who have watched its growth through the years first go over to check its health, then get down to the business that brought them to the office.

In the early days we took what accounts we could get— glass containers, hardware, keys, flower-show exhibits, cedar chests, department-store window displays, bottles, hinges, children's furniture, a line of pianos.

I wrote countless letters to big men in industry, hoping to indoctrinate them into the mysteries and advantages of industrial design. Looking back, I think the direct, personal approach of these letters, which explained our work, assured the recipients we could improve their products and increase their business, and requested an interview, was of great

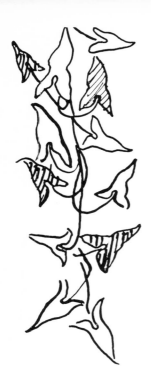

value. We have been retained to this day by some of the friends we first contacted by these letters. A New York Central vice-president was asked by a magazine writer how he happened to employ us. He said, "All I can recall is that at the absolute bottom of the depression, when thousands of perfectly good railway cars were standing idle all over the country, this youngster followed up a sales letter by walking in with a mess of sketches under his arm and talked us into letting him redesign a bunch of cars and then into designing a whole new Twentieth Century Limited."

FROM the outset, I determined to keep our staff small and compact, so we might render a personal service to our clients. As a result, we have restricted our client list to approximately fifteen, sometimes less, depending on the magnitude of the jobs. If this figure seems small, it should not be interpreted to mean that we have time on our hands. On the contrary, our offices in New York and California are beehives. The explanation is that some of our clients may each produce more than one hundred products a year or request us to oversee the design of products made in as many as twenty factories or may have us designing a fleet of transport planes, simultaneously.

Our goal has always been to become a member of the client's "family," remaining in touch with his problems, co-operating closely on his current merchandise, but also keeping a sharp eye out for future programs. We feel that we must be faces and personalities—not merely a voice on the telephone, the signature on a letter, or an initial on a drawing.

Six partners head up the organization. They are supplemented by a hand-picked staff of architects, engineers, designers, artists, and sculptors—each doing the work for which he or she is trained and best suited. Some of these co-workers have been with us for more than twenty years. We also maintain a proportionately large clerical staff, which aids in research, scheduling, and office routine, so that the creative group may be relieved of some of this burden.

We work in close collaboration from the generic design to the finished product. The meeting of schedules, development of designs, and the carrying through process into actual production is the responsibility of the individual partners. They are empowered to hire whatever personnel they need and are in full command of the jobs under their control. On some jobs there is frequent interchange of personnel— members of our staff may work in the client's engineering department, and conversely, we often "borrow" engineers from a client's staff. When we were working on an airplane, we borrowed an engineer from our aeronautical client to help us over some technical hurdles, and it was almost two years later that we realized we'd forgotten to return him!

Geography determines which jobs will be handled by our New York and California offices. Both offices are available to those clients who have factories near both coasts. A careful system of reports on meetings, phone calls, letters, and, of course progress of current designs keeps both offices fully acquainted with details of all jobs. This arrangement leaves me free to "float" between the two offices, and my time is about evenly divided between them. At times I almost live by the airplane schedules.

Frequently, each of the partners is in a different city at a different client's factory on a given day. Or we may all appear at Tulsa, Oklahoma, to visit the oil-industry exhibit on a single day. One of our secretaries totaled the office travel for a year and determined that we had flown over a quarter of a million miles.

No matter where I am, I am kept up to date on all work, so that, if necessary, I may step into any job at any time at any place. I receive a large envelope daily—air mail, special delivery—full of vital statistics: correspondence, memos, reports, drawings, photographs of models, blueprints, and samples of materials.

We subscribe to scores of publications, which are available to all staff members. Like our research trips through department stores, they help keep us abreast of the times, not only in this country but abroad. Any facts we encounter in these publications which might relate to a client's business are promptly sent to him.

WE search incessantly for new ideas, new methods, new materials. We are not content to stand still or to accept present processes as the final word. If we are to progress, we must constantly evaluate the *status quo*, and if what it stands for is no longer valid, we must abandon it. We look for new points of view, new perspectives. We have found that the creative process is stimulated by new experience and new knowledge.

We have no pat phrase for what makes our organization tick. Perhaps the secret, if it is a secret, lies in a sincere interest in what we are doing and persistence to an end. To put it another way, our greatest incentive is our desire to create the best possible designs and then see them get on the market. After all, at the end of each year, we can measure our progress only by the products of our clients that have found acceptance with Joe and Josephine.

All this is true of all good industrial-design offices. The specific methods described here may be peculiar to our operation, but the basic goals and concepts are universal.

CHAPTER 18. RE-APPRAISAL

WHEN the first edition of *Designing for People* was published in 1955, it seemed logical, appropriate and easy to wind up with some speculations about life at the close of the second half of the twentieth century. After all, it's part of the industrial designer's business—as I noted then—to let his thoughts roam, to dream a little, to look ahead in time to the beginnings of Century 21 when, doubtless, today's sleek designs will seem quaintly amusing to our great-grandchildren.

At that time, I could tick off, without the least twinge of concern that my own educated hunches about tomorrow would have come and gone, a respectable list of things we might reasonably expect.

Rereading that original "appraisal," I'm now amazed and humbled by how many "speculations" that in 1955 I feared might seem too far out are realities. My crystal-gazing wasn't too radical. It was too conservative—in timing if not in concept.

The Picturephone that lets us see as well as speak and listen, on a person-to-person basis, across entire continents . . . closed circuit TV (in full color, at that) . . . heliports to receive heli-taxis in the heart of our great cities . . . application of the atom's power for everyday commerce and industry and medicine . . . all these have come about in barely ten years. And so has travel

214

in space which, in 1955, I prophesied with the loophole clause: ". . . Perhaps, by the end of the second half of the twentieth century . . ."

In 1955, it was not too bold to dream of Buck Rogers come to life and earthships venturing to the moon or Mars or Venus in fifty years. But who would have dared to seriously predict all this in less than ten years—in less than five!

As I sit down once again to look ahead, I feel all too keenly the difficulties in applying a timetable to the sweep of technology, invention and innovation. We can and must try to visualize the world ahead. And we can and must plot the zones of the unknown waiting for the mind's assault. But we should, and again—indeed must—not be surprised at the speed of transformation.

Even the boldest dreamer, backed by the most educated hunches, needs to be prepared for things no one today can logically predict. Just as in the first half of our century we couldn't guess the conquest of the atom's inner space, other conquests will come to pass that right now are beyond the ken of any living man.

But isn't this precisely the industrial designer's dish of tea? New machines and new materials will almost literally explode from our laboratories and workshops. The human mind itself will have as an awesome handmaiden The Computer, which turns one second into the equivalent of thirty years' normal time. This even has a name: the nano-second, which already has replaced the micro-second which made one second equal to three weeks.

For all this, one thing is certain. Joe and Josephine, the indestructible, will wander through this panorama, be it amazing or simply a maze. How they act, what they think, what they feel, will be a development, an extension, of how they act, think and feel today.

For the industrial designer, the job is already assigned; to fit the new machines and materials—whatever they may be, whenever they appear—to people. The industrial designer's task is still to relate the inanimate with the animate, to improve, if you'll forgive the conceit, a world of non-designer people, non-designer machines and non-designed things, the things you bump your head on and bang your shins on, the things that gum up, waste space, cost too much to make, cost even more to maintain, and are ugly to boot.

These are today's villains and they'll still be villains tomorrow. In fact, the technological sweep, moving in nano-second time, may make them more numerous and unpleasant than they have been so far. One half-perfected idea can be multiplied a billion times, packaged, shipped and made part of a mass marketing campaign before you can say, "Josephine." Or even "Joe." But, fortunately the same speedy techniques are applicable to *good* design—and good design can be spread at equal speed.

Knowing full well that some of the predictions I am about to make may conceivably take place before the ink is dry on the manuscript, and with considerable trepidation, I share some

216

of my future dreaming with you.

IN THE AIR

How are we going to get around? Supersonic flight is an accomplished fact and the question arises of how much faster we really want to go, particularly when audio and visual communication continues to improve. What we do have to consider is what super-speed will be doing to us.

Somehow, our metabolism is going to have to adjust to fast change. Flying from New York to Los Angeles, we will arrive at our destination 1½ hours before we take off from our point of departure—and, much worse, the 6-hour time change between Paris and New York means we will arrive in New York 4 hours before we left Paris. How do we explain this to our stomachs and our sleeping habits? Some new type of edible "time capsule" will have to be devised—color-coded for the number of hours and meals it agrees to absorb.

With miracle fabrics being constantly improved, we will be able to take an uncrushable wardrobe, packed in a small bag and tucked under our seats. There will be no waiting at our destination for baggage delivery.

For the man or woman on the run, airports will be selling such luggage all pre-packed and including all necessities; you will state merely the length of your trip, the size of your waist, your color preference and the climate of your destination.

Limited personal flight, already accomplished by our armed forces, will be available to all of us. By standing on the platform of a hover craft or harnessing ourselves into a contraption, we will soar above the earth (a radar will prevent our colliding with the other angels) and after all, there IS a lot of room up there.

ON THE RAILS

The Renaissance of the Rails is about to overtake us. The Federal government has backed up with millions of dollars its belief that surface transportation between large metropolises is a necessity. When you travel by air you must reckon adding to your hours aloft the time consumed in getting to and from the airport. When you compare this total to a trip by train speeding at 300 miles an hour, from and to terminals located in the heart of a city, the railroad makes a great deal of sense—and it is practically weather-resistant.

We are already exploring new ways to propel trains; soon we will get rid of the nuisance and noise of wheels. Strong magnets will be employed to repel the vehicle and hold it suspended, as it "floats" on a cushion of air. Propulsion thru a tube may make use of a longitudinal motor—the tube being the field and the car replacing the rotor—and speed again increased.

From door to door, in many instances, rail time will beat air time.

ON THE ROAD

Bad dreams are caused by traffic jams. 1.8 persons travel in the average car designed to accommodate six; our freeways and parkways and turnpikes, reportedly the finest in the world, become impotent bumper-to-bumper parking lots at commuting time.

We need a car to fit the single daily commuter, but at the push of a button on the dashboard, it will expand to take care of the family on weekends.

Safety, today's hue and cry of the automotive world, should have been its first consideration years ago. Automatic pilots on cars will release us from the burden and boredom of watching the road, and will protect everyone from the other fellow's carelessness, for radar-operated brakes will be employed in man-controlled as well as automatic driving. A collision or pile-up of cars will become impossible. As one vehicle approaches another or, for that matter, as a vehicle faces any solid matter, the radar eye will operate the brakes.

THE LAND

In 1866, it took one man and his horse 4 hours to till one acre of land; modern farm machinery plows an acre in 10 minutes. The engineers who accomplished this time-saving machinery will continue to advance the art.

Means will be found to convert energy directly into work and, the sharp steel cultivators that can be cruel to tender plants will be supplanted by an electronic device that will gently stir the soil; in a matter of seconds a farm of hundreds of acres will be cultivated by the flip of a switch.

UNDER THE SEA

Seven-tenths of the Earth's surface is covered by water— much of it of unfathomable depths; we have still to conquer the seas. And eventually, our population explosion will crowd us to a point where we will be forced to live and work under the water.

Some of us will embrace the idea of living, playing and working in the cool depths, enjoying the colorful underwater-scape through the oversized picture porthole of our submerged home. In the filtered light from above, we will enjoy magnificent foliage against a background of great formations of coral and fish; crustacea of unbelievable forms and colors will populate the area. We will go for a "walk" with our pet dolphin. (Of course, it will never rain!) We will leave our homes for visiting, working or going to school, either in the family-size submarine or, if we choose, we will don mask and tanks and turn on our personalized propeller—which is much safer than trying personal flight through the air.

Whole factories will be built on the ocean floor, deriving power from the tides and changes in temperature. Sea-growing plants will provide raw materials to be manufactured into products. Fish attracted to an underwater factory, will be caught and instantly frozen for the gourmets still living on terra firma.

And what of the harvest of the sea? Seaweed already fortifies ice cream, and the Japanese enhance our gourmet habits with delectable hors d'oeuvres derived from seaweed. This is only the small beginning of the crops that will come from the sea and stave off starvation for our multiplying population.

The ingenuity of the men who provide us with mechanical devices to plow, sow, fertilize, cultivate and harvest the land will surely develop machines to handle the enormous crops we will grow on the ocean's floor.

THE WEATHER

The statement that "Everyone talks about the weather but nobody does anything about it" will no longer be true. Satellites will report weather threats long before they occur, and we will prepare for them and so avert disaster.

Furthermore, we will learn to control weather. We will conjure up fair skies for a garden wedding or seed clouds with silver-iodide to bring a downpour to parched wheatfields. I hope our agriculturists will put this to good use but, at frightening worst, one warring country could relentlessly inflict rain, snow or scorching heat upon its enemy. Crops could be inundated or burned. Such misfortune could be a worse catastrophe than an atomic attack.

On the brighter side of weather control, our cities would be air conditioned and the air purified inside and outside our buildings, and lighted at our command by an artificial sun. This would mean a minimum of clothing the year round, and if we wished the temperature in New York, Chicago and London could be identical to Los Angeles, Miami and Honolulu.

THE WORLD AROUND US

If we could start from scratch, surely we would not crowd our cities with block after block of skyscraper canyons. Imagine a city plan like a giant checkerboard: high rise buildings on the black squares and grass and trees on the red ones. Below the grass areas of the checkerboard, underground banks, computer centers, supermarkets, stores, parking areas and libraries. The space above would be landscaped and enhanced with sculpture and pools, a gift of space and light and air to the community.

THE HOUSE

Bringing water, gas, electricity and communication services to a home involves a major financial outlay. One day we will have a self-sufficient house. It will be factory-built and delivered by a flying sky crane; the site can be as remote as desired, for no connections to the usual services will be necessary. A small nuclear plant will furnish power for light, heat, cooling, cooking and home entertainment. The telephone will operate on microwave. When the house is completed a sufficient amount of water will be flown in, the amount depending on your needs, and the water will be used and reused, chemically purified, the waste matter being removed and converted into fertilizer for your garden. Transportation, if you ever choose to leave this Shangri-la, will be via light plane, capable of vertical takeoff and landing, or by helicopter or personal flight.

Our needs for useable space constantly change. A couple getting started want a minimum area. When they produce a family, they require additional room. Eventually, their children move away and there is a need for shrinkage of the premises.

Homes built on a module system could be added to with ease. The future homeowner will select an additional room from a catalogue, a phone call will bring the room via sky-crane which will set it exactly where it is wanted; (hook-up for utilities and access are part of the original structure). Years later, when less space is required, another phone call will again summon a helicopter, the room will be unbuckled from the house and flown to the "used room-lot" and be available to the next customer.

FURNISHINGS

Perhaps there would be more serenity if our surroundings were less cluttered. We will avoid over-crowded rooms by adding inflatable furniture to accommodate extra guests. Via carbon dioxide capsules, chairs will appear only when needed, and be folded away when the guests depart.

We are all aware that people come in all sorts of shapes and sizes and, yet, we never try to fit a chair to a particular person —we just take what comes along. The seats in our automobiles respond to button operation—they go up and down, forward and backward and even recline. Why not have a comfort control panel in the arm of an easy chair in our own homes that

222

would do all of those things and more, too? It could also make the chair harder or softer to suit the user, and certainly it could include a built-in reading light, and sound reception audible only to the occupant.

Though we toss our underclothes into the wash after one wearing, why doesn't it bother us to sleep between the same bedsheets every night for a week? (We would be aghast at spending 56 hours in the same underwear, but that's what we do with bed linens.) Luxuriously soft and disposable cellulose sheets would be more satisfactory—a dozen of them fastened together at the top—one to be torn off and thrown away each morning. *Thus would a pad become a "pad."*

MAN WORKS FROM SUN TO SUN BUT WOMEN'S WORK IS NEVER DONE

This is another old adage that will not survive! Automation in the office, in the factory, in construction and in farming is bound to liberate men; our five-day work week will be reduced to a four- and for some even a three-day week of labor. Man, given all of this additional leisure time will want to share it with his wife and family. But if the ladies are to provide additional companionship for their leisure-rich husbands, they, too, must reduce their work hours. How can they be helped?

Houses will be provided with an entry-way or vestibule that will subsonically remove dirt particles from shoes, clothing and from exposed parts of your body. Thus, cleaning the interior of the house will be reduced to a minimum—and what is still necessary will be done electrostatically, continuously attracting dirt to a central point and then flushing it away.

Kitchens and bathrooms requiring constant cleaning will be

formed of a single seamless unit with no cracks to harbor dirt. The floors will be flushed with a detergent and rinsed by the push of a button.

Automated cooking will come into the home. There will be a refrigstove-combo; the insertion of a card holding a preferred menu will start the combo working. Out of a deep freeze, the selected foods in the quantities requested will travel to a defrosting unit, then to a cooking unit and finally to the table. "Cleaning up" will be accomplished by placing the used dishes in the dish closet. At the push of a button they will be washed and sterilized and put neatly on their shelves, ready for the next meal.

For a quick snack, a plug-in package! On the outside of the package which contains prepared food, there will be a disposable electric plug to heat the contents.

Like the portable typewriter, computers are already approaching home size, and will be just as essential to family happiness. Encyclopedic information, family histories, recipes—all will be stored and ready to be called forth when required. Perhaps the computer will store a list of our friends; including each person's interests, background and personality. When we give a party, compatible guests will be assembled and, of course, the computer will provide a menu differing from those of their previous visits.

DISPOSABLE

An ice cream cone is a perfect package! It displays the merchandise; it allows you to see, feel, smell and taste it. The entire product is happily disposed of by the time you are through with it. But few things are so obliging and there are few on earth, including our own bodies, that do not leave some residue.

Eight hundred million pounds of trash and garbage turn up every day in the United States. A good deal of it is burned, or used as land fill—and this either pollutes the air we breathe or the water we drink. Gradually we are seeing the light of day, and communities are agitating to make an asset out of this liability by building plants that will turn refuse into fertilizer.

In Los Angeles county alone, there are eighteen billion, nine hundred million pounds of waste generated annually! (*To bring down to human scale, this means that every man, woman and child produces an average of 2700 pounds of waste every year.*)

Think of all the vitamins that go down the disposals in our kitchens; if nothing else, they could be combined into an efficient fertilizer. More and more food comes in packages; why can't the package be edible and be part of the food?

In the future, the waste products of our civilization that pollute the air and water around us will be converted into useful materials or will be self-destroying.

(And, in a lighter vein, I want an edible toothpick, flavored with celery, olive or onion, to stab snacks and olives at cocktail parties and so relieve my pockets of the telltale wooden staves that collect there.)

TELEVISION

The most terrifying object on today's scene is TV. Buckminster Fuller has said that since every child has three parents —two natural ones and the TV set—why can't that parent be a good one?

To my mind, television is more important than the invention of movable type. One needs no learning to sit in front of the hypnotic "boob tube" and succumb to the insidious pap that is spooned from it. But think of the wonders that might enter our classrooms and our living rooms and our souls via this medium; painlessly, we could educate every man, woman and child in the universe.

Long before school, our children, at an age when they most easily absorb knowledge, will be inculcated with an ear for music and eye for art. They will get the rudiments of mathematics and languages, their curiosity will be whetted for travel and the beginnings of astronomy and biology; that could be a worthy substitute for the one-eyed nursemaid of the modern home that today deals out horror stories and breeds nightmares instead of sweet dreams.

The miracle of television will be expanded. We will sit in a room and, at the flick of a switch, the walls and ceiling will disappear—all becoming a single screen. We will truly be on a magic carpet. Stereophonic sound will complete our illusion of being in another environment, and will transport us to the center of Elsinore to see a fine performance of Hamlet, or if you prefer, to the Yale-Harvard game; we will be "in" the picture surrounded by color and sound.

And this technique, via telephone, will be used for personal communications. A visit with grandchildren—in full size, full color and *full noise*—will be possible. Shopping will be done from an armchair, whether for a roast or a new dress; and we need not be confined to local stores; one may live in New York and select a new gown in Dallas, or vice versa.

Instantaneously we will summon a business conference with colleagues from several lands, each sitting in his own office, seeing and talking to us as we see and talk to them.

SCHOOL?

A population explosion, of necessity, starts with the very

young. Between now and the year 2000 A.D., 139,702,200 babies will be born.

Of course, they must all be educated, but is it necessary to be so old-fashioned as to think they must attend school every day? Will our land space have room to accommodate that many school buildings? And it would take a line of buses as long as that once proverbial trip to the moon for transportation to and from school.

But most important—where are the teachers to come from?

President Garfield expressed his ideal of a perfect teaching environment: "My definition of a university is Mark Hopkins at one end of a log and a student at the other."

The concept of sufficient genius pedagogues, and enough logs to accommodate them and our extra millions of students, is clearly an unattainable goal. Failing to provide the necessary number of live teachers for all our future population, we must add electronic devices.

A computer can teach facts and figures, record each student's progress unemotionally, and relieve the live teacher of thousands of time-consuming tasks. Periodically, it will combine its stored-up knowledge of each student's aptitudes with the live teacher's judgments and advise what future education and even what profession or trade the student should pursue. (Somehow, the computer will even detect the late bloomer and hold out for continuing education.)

We are familiar with TV as used in the classroom and the advantages of an outstanding instructor-performer appearing on hundreds of screens simultaneously. It takes little stretch of the imagination and no new electronic art to multiply those screens by millions and have the same instructor appear in each of our homes.

There will be a *"learning room"* in every home to be used by students in the daytime and available for adult education after hours. It will be equipped with every conceivable audio and visual aid, connected via coaxial cable, microwave, telephone wire or laser beam to central teaching headquarters. Already in existence are computer-based machines (in use at Stanford University) to which a student via Teletype keyboard may direct a question and receive an immediate and indisputable answer.

An effective and satisfactory balance of time will be arrived at so as to permit the face-to-face teacher to contribute to the all-important creative areas and provide inspiration, encouragement and sympathetic understanding to combat the contrasting cold, factual, unemotional output of the efficient electronic master.

And planning for the future, a fringe benefit is at hand, since in a new age every emerging student will have a total familiarity with electronics and the now friendly computer which he will most certainly be using and depending upon for the rest of his days.

COMPUTERS

Today, no big business could operate effectively without a computer, and we all admit they have speeded up matters in an extraordinary and efficient manner. We have seen a computer take a plan and two elevations and from this information instantaneously project a perspective on a screen; and then, when ordered, revolve that perspective in all directions as though it were in three dimensions.

Certainly, all of the data we have on human engineering, once in a computer, can test any product accurately, quickly—

and the answers are incontestable.

But here, I call a halt. The assumption that creative design can be developed via this machanical brain is utter nonsense. No machine can be creative, original, imaginative—and certainly it cannot be an arbiter of taste. There is something that I hope creators have between their two ears that just cannot be put on tape and wound around reels.

We are learning to live with and to appreciate the computer and, as with any other tool, we will learn to do some things faster or better. But, as *designers*, we can never surrender that one uniquely human quality of mind to some electronic *Wunderkind*—the intuitive, creative "flash of insight," the inner thunderclap of revelation that tells us our answer to a problem is right.

The wheel, a wondrous invention in its time, liberated man; movable type opened his eyes; steam propelled him around the world, but, in one fell swoop, a little black box full of transistors and relays, generators and printed circuits has gone to work for him and has given him leisure. The rapid progress of automation, transportation and communication is creating additional time faster than we know how to use it. Will these extra hours be waste or gain? Will the entire population be educated as Shakespearean scholars or study higher mathematics—or will it resort to TV who-dunits and comic books?

Will we use our new freedom to improve our bodies as well as our minds? (And, if a healthy body makes a healthy mind, the more exercise and sporting activities we engage in, the more intellectuals we will develop!)

How can we be stimulated in the right direction? With everything around us being machine-made, will an urge arise for "do-it-yourself" projects; will we become dressmakers, carpenters, potters? Perhaps some of us will use our sunny leisure hours to become horticultural experts and make the whole world a garden. "Sunday Painters" will be a misnomer, for we will have time to try our palette and brush every day of the week. All of those books we've promised ourselves to read, all of the music we've wanted to hear—all are waiting for us and our new-found hours.

Somehow, we must find again our sense of individual values, lost in this century of enormous technological advance. This very freedom that mechanical aids are giving us has welded us into unmanageable megalopolises, where people are anonymous numbers and where communication with our fellow man seems a minus quantity. We must restore the warmth and spirit we had in the smaller community. I hope that, in our leisure time we will once again know our neighbor—and if everyone knows his neighbor and learns to live with him, the entire world will be at peace.

There are dozens—hundreds of things—worthwhile or wasteful—we can do in our extra time. But first we should set aside a small portion of our new leisure to examine the way we live our lives. Unless we improve upon it we will just be repeating our old worn-out habits. Perhaps A. A. Milne was really addressing us rather than our children when he wrote; "Here is Edward Bear, coming downstairs now, bump, bump, bump, on the back of his head, behind Christopher Robin. It is, as far as he knows, the only way of coming downstairs, but sometimes he feels that there really is another way, if only he could stop bumping for a moment and think of it."